Successful Single Parenting

Gary Richmond

HARVEST HOUSE PUBLISHERS
Eugene, Oregon 97402

SUCCESSFUL SINGLE PARENTING

Copyright © 1990 by Harvest House Publishers
Eugene, Oregon 97402

Library of Congress Cataloging-in-Publication Data

Richmond, Gary, 1944-
    Successful single parenting / Gary Richmond.
    ISBN 0-89081-768-5
        1. Single parents—United States—Life skills guides.   I. Title.
    HQ759.915.R54   1989   89-31531
    306.85'6--dc20   CIP

Printed in the United States of America.

TO BUCK BUCHANAN

Buck cares for the needs
of the brokenhearted.
He is the kind of man and minister
I would like to be.
He is my friend.
This work is dedicated to him.

Contents

Acknowledgements

In Gratitude

I would like to thank the following people:
— The members of my Single Parent Fellowship for their help on this work. They established the curriculum with their own lives. They shared what they would like to see in a manuscript such as this and often provided the answers to the hardest questions by the way they were living their lives.

— Chuck Swindoll for allowing me to use a chapter from *Improving Your Serve* (Word Books). The Forgiveness chapter is the finest part of this book. Chuck is wonderful to work for because he is godly, encouraging, practical, creative, fair, caring, inspiring, strong, fun and a shepherd to his staff. He is a wonderful model and the finest boss I have ever served under.

— Marsi Beauchamp, Travis and Jeanette Bollen and Dick and Naomi Landorf. They are coworkers in our single-parents ministry and the ones to whom I go most often to ask the question, "What is the best way to deal with this problem?" They are always willing to think and serve, and I treasure their friendship and counsel.

— Annie Husman, my secretary, for her fine work and consistently sweet spirit. Her enthusiasm and spark is part of what makes serving at Evangelical Free Church a joy.

— Word Books, Inc., for permitting me to use a chapter from my book *The Divorce Decision* and a chapter from Chuck Swindoll's book *Improving Your Serve*. The people at Word are more than business associates, they are friends and coworkers in the ministry.

— My friends over at Joybells Bible Bookstore, across the street from the Evangelical Free Church in Fullerton, CA. Eric Ehrman and Roger Pierce are always ready to help me and aided Eric Dunkerley in compiling the Bibliography found in the Appendices.

— I am indebted to Eric Dunkerley for compiling the Bibliography list found in the Appendices.

— Grand thanks to Lela Gilbert for polishing and rearranging this manuscript so that it would be smoother and softer for all who read it. I am deeply in her debt.

— Special thanks to Barbara Gordon for her fine editing work on this manuscript.

—A special thank-you to Eileen Mason, Editor-in-Chief, at Harvest House. Her kindness, patience, interest and encouragement were an example to me. I was extended grace and for that I will be forever thankful. Everyone at Harvest House was wonderful to work with. Bob Hawkins has assembled a terrific staff. The heart of a servant spirit abounds there.

1

Going It Alone—
One Family's Story

Susan Teal sat in her living room staring out the window. Her feet were on the couch, her arms holding her knees close to her body. Thinking about the last year of her life, she slowly rocked back and forth.

The year before had shattered every "happily ever after" dream Susan had ever cherished. The course of her life had been changed forever. Who could have predicted her husband Bob would decide that a younger, more attractive woman was the answer to his unfulfilled longings? Oh, she had felt him slipping away from her at times, but she hadn't expected the worst to happen. Then, once she had realized things were seriously amiss, nothing she had done seemed to alleviate his dissatisfaction. Finally, one terrible day, sitting right there in the living room, he had filled her ears with an unoriginal and all-too-often-delivered speech.

"Susan I don't know exactly how to tell you this. But, well . . . I'm filing for a divorce. You've probably suspected that I've been with another woman. If so, you were right. I haven't been happy for a long time and Ginger... that's her name... she makes me feel alive again. Susan, I want you to know, nothing was really your fault. I know you tried to be a good wife but... I guess it just isn't working for us."

Numbness had paralyzed every part of Susan's body. She hadn't believed what she was hearing.

Bob had continued in a detached and businesslike tone. "I don't want you to worry about whether I'm going to be fair. I know the kids will do better with you, but I hope you will let me see them. I mean, you won't try to punish me for leaving, will you? I still love them, but I don't want to be worrying about all the details. My lawyer will be contacting you. He's suggested that you retain a lawyer of your own as soon as possible."

By now some of the numbness was giving way to anger. "That's it?" Susan had snapped. "It's over, get a lawyer, keep the kids? That's it?"

He had looked away from her as she went on. "Bob, we've been married for 16 years! Don't you think I deserve a chance to do something to save our marriage? We need help! I know you haven't been happy, but you're not the first male to go through a mid-life crisis. It's just something you get over. Please... don't throw away 16 years! Don't crush your children. Bob, they deserve better than this, and so do I. I've had to put up with your distance and neglect for years, but I've hung in there with you. Is this my reward? Tell me, why we can't see a counselor, or a pastor or someone who could help? I feel so lost...."

Bob had coldly replied, "Well, I knew I could count on you for drama!"

"Drama! Bob, it's our marriage!"

"Well, the marriage is over. It's been over for years! In fact, to tell you the truth, I'm not sure if we ever had anything going. We got married too young. We got married because it was the thing to do. You wanted it. My mother wanted it. Your mother wanted it, so who was I not to want it? It seemed like the right thing to do at the time. The truth is, when we were standing in front of Pastor Burch, I wanted to say, 'Wait! I'm too young! I'm not sure about this!' But I kept my mouth shut because I didn't want to hurt or embarrass any of you."

"Good grief, Bob. I hope you're not looking for a kindness award! Sixteen years ago you could have walked away from me. Now you're walking away from a whole family!"

"Yeah, Susan. Right. I guess I knew you'd be unreasonable. Like I said, you'll be hearing from my lawyer. For your information, I'm moving in with Ginger, and I don't want you to call me except in an emergency. Ginger has an unlisted number so I've signed up with an answering service. If there's an emergency with the children just have me paged, and I'll get back to you."

With that Bob handed her the answering service number and walked out the door. If he hadn't avoided her eyes, he would have seen the first of countless tears Susan would cry in the days and weeks to come.

Now, 11 months later, it seemed that the tears had finally dried up. The divorce had just been finalized. All along, Susan had assumed that things would be better once the fighting was over.

Some things were. At least there were more things in the "known" than in the "unknown" column. By now she was fully aware of her not-so-satisfactory financial status. She understood her secretarial salary plus the court-ordered support was barely enough for survival. Nevertheless, Susan was determined to make it.

Fortunately, her supervisor had been through a nasty divorce himself, and was not only understanding but very supportive. He had even suggested she take that particular day off, since it would have been her 17th wedding anniversary. That's how she found herself at home in the middle of the week, looking out the window and remembering the passing of so many difficult days.

Susan's feelings for Bob were dead—at least her love was. By now she wouldn't allow him to come back if he wanted to. (She had no reason to believe that he did.) For months her love for him had been transforming itself into intense and unabated anger. She found herself hating him more than she ever felt she could hate anyone. Besides rejecting her and the children, he had forced her into being single at 38, a fate she would have never chosen for herself.

One night she'd heard noises in the backyard. Was the house being broken into? She had been immobilized with fear. All she could think of doing was pulling the covers over her face and sobbing uncontrollably into the pillow. She was later to learn the source of the sounds— at three o'clock in the morning, her next-door neighbor had been searching through his trash for a lost receipt! Despite the harmless outcome, the incident had produced many restless nights, resulting in a prescription of sleeping pills.

Fear of things that "go bump in the dark" was only one of many qualities Susan didn't like about being single—and a single parent. She had no time for herself. She resented filling out forms that asked "married or divorced?" because they made her feel like a failure. She dreaded seeing old friends that didn't yet know her husband had thrown her away like a used article of clothing. She was humiliated when men looked at her ring finger and "came on" to her, assuming that she desperately needed what they were so very willing to give her.

But most of all, Susan hated what she saw happening to her children.

Jeff had cried a lot at the beginning. Now Susan was receiving notes from his sixth-grade teacher, complaining that he was causing trouble in class. Jeff had never before been a behavior problem. Now he was disruptive both at school and at home. At 12, he was almost more than she could handle.

Charlyn, who was 16, had become bitterly angry and pessimistic. She spent far too much time in her room absorbed in "MTV," only coming out for an occasional Coke or to answer the phone. Come to think of it, Charlyn hadn't been getting as many phone calls lately. Susan vaguely wondered why.

It would have been difficult for Susan to say what she disliked most about her situation. But three issues loomed large in her mind: loneliness; a nagging sense that she had failed; and personal rejection by the one person in the world that knew her best. These matters continually caused her to resent Bob. Try as she might, she had not been able to forgive him. Meanwhile, her own mother's one nagging question haunted her: "What did Bob want from you that you didn't give him, sweetheart? Why did he feel a need to look for someone else?"

Susan had tortured herself trying to answer. "Well, she can have him," Susan finally concluded. "I don't really want him anymore." Probably, more accurately, she would have liked having him back just long enough to reject him. Then maybe he would better understand the agony he had put her through.

Susan was unbelievably tired at night when she returned home from work. Part of the exhaustion stemmed from the realization that she was merely two-thirds of the way through her day. She had tried to get the kids to take some responsibility around the house, but had been unsuccessful. By now she had succumbed to the belief that it was easier to do all the work herself than to force them to help.

She was usually greeted by Jeff, lying on the couch, an assortment of junk food spread in front of him on the coffee table. His jogging shoes were here and there, his school books in the middle of the floor along with his backpack. Her greeting to him was rarely warm, because she knew what he would most certainly ask next: "What's for dinner, Mom?"

Invariably, she responded, "Have you started your homework?"

This was countered by, "Get off my case, Mom! You know I can't do homework when I'm starving to death!"

Jeff rarely even looked up when he was talking to her. "All in the Family" reruns were what really mattered to him. There were times when Susan almost wished she could start life all over again without her children. She was deeply worried that they were not going to turn out well. Trapped in her own struggles, she didn't seem to have the resources to help them win the battle for health and good character. Their self-centeredness frightened her. Their deep needs seemed impossible to fill. And all the while, her own loneliness ached painfully inside her.

Susan was in a dilemma. She felt desperately alone. But what if she went out socially? Her children would be unsupervised, and she was quite sure they would not handle the additional free time well. They already arrived home three hours before she did. True, Charlyn was 16, but Susan didn't think her already troubled daughter should have to deal with Jeff's newly acquired sarcasm and explosive temperament.

Besides, where would she go? And with whom?

Susan and Bob had once been active in their church, until he had decided "everybody is phony there." She had continued for a while, but had felt awkward explaining Bob's absence. So, other than Sunday morning services, she had quit going too.

Their church was very strict in its views about divorce, causing Susan to feel self-conscious whenever she attended. Once, during a particularly difficult time, she had sought the pastor out for a word of encouragement. He had seemed genuinely to care, and he did try to communicate that God loved her and would provide for her. But then he'd spoiled it all by spending the last 30 minutes emphasizing her need to avoid temptation. "Remember," he had warned, "that until the divorce is final, you're still a married woman. You should not be seen in the company of men. And if you'll pray with all your heart, maybe God will bring Bob back."

Susan hadn't had the heart to tell the pastor that she no longer wanted Bob back! So after they prayed together she left, more troubled than before, more defeated and guilty than when she had arrived.

Going it alone was not Susan's cup of tea. Still, like it or not, she could only attempt to make the best of it. Other people had made it through. In time so would she. But that didn't stop her from wishing someone would show her a short cut!

Jeff didn't like going it alone either. He loved his mother and his father, and he wasn't sure who to blame for the family's break up. When he asked his mother why she and Dad were getting a divorce Susan said, "I think you'll have to ask your father that question because I don't know either."

When Jeff asked his father, he was given a vague description of a marriage that never should have occurred. What Jeff heard was that his father had tried for years to "make it work," but it never did. Bob's explanation made the divorce sound like a mutual decision—he and Susan just couldn't put their marriage together.

For the longest time, every day at 6:30 P.M., Jeff stared at the front door, hoping his father would come home from work as he always had. Needless to say, it never happened. Bob had raised Jeff to believe that when things went wrong it was somebody's fault. That concept frustrated the boy. It made him angry, because he couldn't figure out who was to blame.

He sometimes entertained the theory that his mother must not have been nice enough to his father, so he'd left to find someone else. Jeff still didn't know that Ginger had been a part of his father's life long before the divorce occurred. Sometimes Jeff raged at Bob for not trying harder to return.

Jeff's underlying conviction was that if he had been a better son, his father would never have gone away. He wondered what he might have done to cause this horrible turn of events. Many nights he cried quietly into his pillow, begging God to "bring Daddy home."

Sadly, Daddy never came.

Did his parents know he was hurting? Jeff was too embarrassed to share his pain with friends. And adults just couldn't be trusted. But somehow, he needed to be noticed. He needed attention. And it wasn't long before he found ways to get it.

He found that when he talked during class and failed to do his homework, his teachers spent more time with him. He really enjoyed being told how smart he was and what he could accomplish if he tried. He enjoyed anyone caring enough to spend time with him.

He also discovered that he could get more attention from his mother if he made things difficult for her. Yet the attention he was receiving failed to make him happy. Even the thrill of stealing a Nintendo game from the computer store had only taken his mind off his hurt for a short while.

Jeff enjoyed seeing his father every other weekend. What he didn't enjoy was sharing him with Ginger and her daughter Amber. Amber was seven and, by Jeff's standards, rather spoiled. Her favorite expression was, "That's mine!" She said it so often that Jeff never felt at home in Ginger's apartment.

Ginger was nice enough to him, but he resented her telling him what to do. After all, she wasn't his real mother. Authority was for real moms and dads and schoolteachers and principals. Ginger didn't qualify in any category. She was just his father's girlfriend, and that didn't mean much to Jeff. The fact was, he wished his father didn't have one at all.

The holidays had been a nightmare. On Christmas, Jeff found himself whisked to four locations. Christmas morning he ate breakfast at home with his mom and Charlyn. The presents he opened were nowhere near what he had once enjoyed. He tried his best not to show his disappointment, but he could see sadness in his mother's eyes when he didn't show any enthusiasm for the sweater she had bought him. She had cautioned him before that Christmas wouldn't be quite the same. But clothes instead of fun gifts just didn't cut it.

At 10:00 A.M., Bob had picked him up and they had gone to Ginger's apartment. Jeff didn't fare much better there. It was clear that Bob had given Amber gifts just as nice as Jeff's. He was hurt, because he wanted to be more special than Amber. He was glad when they left for his Grandmother's house but felt frustrated that Amber would be horning in on that also.

Grandma didn't seem to care a great deal for Ginger or Amber. But Jeff was never alone with her long enough to ask. She was one of the few people whom he trusted, however he didn't know if she would want to talk about personal things. Grandma had always catered to her son Bob, but that day she almost seemed glad when it was time for him and his new "family" to go.

Next Jeff was delivered to Susan's parents. Grandma Sarah was his favorite cook and she had fixed all of his favorite dishes. Grandma and Grandpa had even bought him a fun gift—something he wanted but didn't need. By the end of the day, Jeff was exhausted. And he wasn't sure why, but he cried himself to sleep that night. He was too young to understand that he was mourning the passing of "what Christmas used to be." Christmas would never be the same.

Never again.

Of all the Teals, Charlyn had been the most radically affected by the divorce. Before, she would have been described as a gentle, compliant and gracious 16-year-old girl. That description was no longer appropriate.

New adjectives would include withdrawn, cynical, sarcastic and hardened. Charlyn had once spent hours on the phone, but did so no longer. Her friends had grown weary of hearing her complain about everything. They were also a little embarrassed by the way that she treated adults in general, and her own mother in particular.

No one could imagine Charlyn's deep anger toward her father. And since he wasn't there to "punish," she was simply punishing everyone else with her rude and obnoxious attitude. Charlyn had not spoken to her father since the day he left. She referred to him as "the jerk," and to Ginger as "the slut."

On one occasion, Susan had corrected her for using such degrading words. Charlyn had blurted out, "The school shrink said that I'm entitled to my feelings and that's the way that I feel." With that, she had stormed out of the kitchen, and had run into her bedroom slamming the door behind her. Charlyn had never shed a tear over the divorce. And she had never allowed anyone else to delve into her feelings.

At the time the divorce was taking place, Charlyn had been going out with a boy named Dirk. Dirk quickly sensed that she was hurt, and was craving more affection than usual. Of course the girl enjoyed feeling close, and the more he held her in his arms and kissed her the better she felt.

One night he pressed for a more intimate relationship. Charlyn was too weak to say "No." Two weeks later she found a break-up letter in her locker, and he hadn't spoken to her since. Young as she was, Charlyn was sadder and wiser. She concluded that men could not be trusted and that life wasn't fair. Her anger for her father raged more fiercely every day. She fervently wished that he would burn in hell for hurting their family so much.

Along with her pain grew a clinical depression. Her eyes looked dull, she had no energy and was losing a lot of weight. MTV dulled her mind, serving as a sort of anesthetic, helping the time pass. As Charlyn lost her focus, everything began to lose value.

Before long, she found a new set of friends at school. Many of them had also experienced the break up of their homes. They seemed to understand life as she did—none of these teenagers saw much point to anything. Many of Charlyn's new friends used drugs, and as far as she was concerned, the idea of getting high sounded like a welcome diversion from her volcanic emotions.

One night she stayed with a girlfriend whose parents were out of town for the weekend. The girls experimented with marijuana and cocaine. For Charlyn, the drug rush was the first real kick she had had since her father walked out the door.

But the pain of his departure had never diminished, no matter how much time went by. Charlyn knew very well that drugs were not the answer. So what was the answer? Drugs would just have to do until she found it! She couldn't afford the amount of drugs she wanted, so she began to trade sexual favors for them. She wasn't a virgin anymore, anyway. What difference did it make?

Charlyn forced herself not to care about anything or anyone. "Caring" simply represented too much risk. Besides, these days she not only had to deal with the divorce, but she was facing other matters of conscience. Worst of all, she had a drug habit whose demonic claws were strangling all the good qualities out of her.

She still loved her mother. But, unintentionally, Susan had withdrawn from her in an attempt to contend with her own pain. Everything her mother asked of her seemed unfair or unreasonable. Drugs had dulled all of Charlyn's coping mechanisms. Her reactions were almost always overreactions—out of proportion to the request being made.

Most of all, whether she knew it or not, she desperately wanted her father to come home and ask her forgiveness for hurting her so much. This was the time of life she needed him most and he wasn't there for her. Clearly, Bob wasn't coming back and Susan wouldn't have him if he did. One night Charlyn imagined that she and Jeff were like Hansel and Gretel. She wasn't sure if they were lost in the woods or being baked in the witch's furnace! Wherever they were, it wasn't any fun and she just wanted to go home. And "home" as she had known it, was forever lost.

Meanwhile, although his family didn't know it, Bob was the most miserable of them all. Nothing was working out quite the way he had imagined.

At the beginning of the relationship, Ginger had helped him feel young again. But now that was wearing off. Forbidden fruit had become a steady diet and the taste had grown bland. The pair had no history, no traditions or memories. Their entire relationship had, more or less, been built on sex, and by now their sex life was rather mundane. They had no close mutual friends. None of Bob's relatives approved of Ginger and he found her relatives boring. He had grown tired of Amber, and was thoroughly disgusted with the way her mother had spoiled her.

Bob sensed a growing distance between himself and Ginger. It would be just a matter of time before he would be moving on, leaving her behind. But where would he go? Bob didn't have an answer to that sobering question.

In the meantime, guilt about his family was eating him alive. He knew that Susan had deserved better from him. She had kept her promises. He hadn't. She hadn't turned her back on every value they had wanted to instill in their children. He had. Would Jeff and Charlyn ever respect him again?

The fact was, he wasn't sure he could ever again respect himself. Nothing would ever be "right" again, and it was clearly his fault. He loved seeing Jeff, but Jeff didn't feel at home when he was at Ginger's. Worse yet, it was evident that Jeff wasn't the carefree son he'd once known.

But the greatest heartbreak was the loss of his daughter, Charlyn. He had never bargained on that. That was the thing that made him cry during the midnight hours, when the important things of the soul beg to be heard. Bob wondered if his sweet Charlyn would ever let him into her life again. It was that anxiety that pressed heaviest against his chest and pounded his brain.

Peace of mind had eluded Bob for months. A canopy of darkness overshadowed him wherever he went. This wasn't the way life was supposed to have worked out! Ginger should have met his needs. His children should have adjusted. The guilt should have evaporated. Instead, all he had to show for his "new life" was a bad dream—a dream from which he wondered if he would ever wake up.

Bob, Susan, Charlyn, Jeff and even Ginger and Amber are all going it alone. Not one of them has it easy, and no magic formulas will ever make their lives a paradise on earth. There are, however, ways for victims of broken homes to make it through.

Read on and you'll find honest facts and figures, spiritual counsel and some down-to-earth practical ideas. These have been written with love, for single parents and their children. Together, we will take a look at some problems and—better yet—some solutions that can make your life more joyful and secure. With God's help, these concepts can lead you on your way to successful single parenting.

2

Extra Baggage

I don't think any task requires more courage and strength than single parenting. It's not just a matter of responsibility. Challenging tasks become far more difficult when we are weighed down by heavy emotional baggage. That baggage is often so cumbersome that it prevents single moms and dads from doing anything effectively—most notably, parenting. Oftentimes, their resources have already been consumed by past struggles, and they have no spare energy left for raising and loving their children.

If you are a single parent, you will no doubt identify with this list of "baggage items" that might be dragging you down:

Self-pity	Anger
Depression	Envy
Guilt	Exhaustion

| Fear | Loneliness |
| Economic devastation | Frustration |

Most single parents are afflicted with many, or most, of those problems. And in working to overcome such painful obstacles, there are no shortcuts. There are no easy answers. Each area must be encountered, explored and left behind.

I know that your goal is to raise healthy, well-adjusted children. That can only be done when you are able to focus on them and not on yourself. Your children are the most precious gifts God has given you, and they need you more now than ever before. So—today is the day to begin shedding the baggage! If you don't, each item will hamper you in a very specific way.

In the motion picture *Clara's Heart,* there is a particularly poignant scene. Clara, a Jamaican nanny played by Whoopie Goldberg, confronts a mother who has lost a baby to death and a husband to an affair. Clara challenges the mother to love her remaining son because he is suffering from neglect as well as from the pain of the divorce. The mother (who is being mentored by a pop psychologist) tells Clara, "I must first be healed myself before I can reach out to my son."

Clara simply says, "That is not true."

Clara is addressing one of our society's greatest lies: "We can only love others to the degree that we love ourselves." Those of us who name Jesus as Lord must remember our calling. Jesus said, "If any man would come after me, let him deny himself and take up his cross and follow me" (Matthew 16:24). Jesus is into self-denial, not self-gratification. That doesn't mean the kind of denial that causes us to avoid truth, for He also teaches that the truth sets us free. The self-denial Jesus talks about involves unselfishness. And it is especially important when children are involved.

The Scriptures teach that the Father will not with-hold any good thing from His children. Nor should we! Therefore, for the children's sake, let's deal with the baggage. But please don't wait until your baggage is gone before you reach out to your sons and daughters. You have more love to give than you realize, and they need it *now*.

And here's a tip, an important principle, an inevitable by-product of your efforts. Your own healing will always be speeded up by the sacrificial love you give to others!

Self-Pity

There is no pitfall along the single parent journey so dark and destructive as self-pity. I have met many men and women who have been mired there for months and years on end. Amazingly enough, it has never done them an ounce of good. The longer one stays lodged in self-pity, the weaker he becomes; the more inwardly focused, the more incapable of loving anyone but him-self.

Everyone is allowed a short episode of self-pity during marital crises, because divorce or abandonment is a severe trial. But once you get your wits about you, climb out of the hole! If you've burrowed in too deeply, you may need to seek help—ask God, and ask your friends and family.

At First Evangelical Free Church of Fullerton, Cali-fornia, where I serve as assistant pastor and oversee the Single Parent Fellowship, we have a divorce recovery program. Our lead teacher, Marsi Beauchamp, shares a great truth with newly-arrived single parents. She ten-derly explains, "To heal more quickly you must 'act' yourself into new feelings—not 'feel' yourself into actions."

I think the apostle Paul was expressing the same idea when he said to be "imitators of God, as beloved chil-dren" (Ephesians 5:1). Children feel brave when they act brave. If you are caught in self-pity's gray web, then determine to make the best of life and refuse to entertain pitiful thoughts. This is an attitude choice you are free to make no matter how difficult your circumstances.

⸤One good test for determining whether you are heavily under the influence of self-pity is found in the answer to this question: How much time do you spend entertaining the thought, "Why me, why now?" The more quickly you simply ask "Lord help me," the more quickly you will begin to heal.⸣

It may be helpful to ask yourself one painful question: To what extent were you responsible for your present situation? Were you caught in an affair? Did you beat your wife? Have you wasted your life with drugs or alcohol? Was everything else more important than your family? If so, then your feelings are consequences, and you can't begin by "acting" yourself into new feelings. That would be a lie. Your road back from self-pity must begin with honest, complete repentance.

If, on the other hand, you know that you are a victim, don't waste your valuable healing time finding ways to blame yourself!

Sometimes we aren't the best assessors of our own circumstances. If you are serious about healing, ask a couple of really close friends if they were aware of things about you that may have caused the downfall of your marriage. Not all of your close friends will believe you can handle criticism, so you may have to ask several people. And by the way, don't let this become an obsession, and once you discover something, simply make note of it. If it's true, repent and move on.

David wrote some profound thoughts on examination of self.

> O Lord, thou hast searched me and known me! Thou knowest when I sit down and when I rise up; thou discernest my thoughts from afar. Thou searchest out my path and my lying

down, and art acquainted with all my ways. Even before a word is on my tongue, lo, O Lord, thou knowest it altogether. Search me, O God, and know my heart! Try me and know my thoughts! And see if there be any wicked way in me, and lead me in the way everlasting! (Psalm 139:1-4,23,24).

Anger

When I was young I remember my father trying his best to fill my head with pithy and wise sayings. I couldn't have been more than 10 when my father said "Son, always remember, 'Hell hath no fury like a woman scorned.'" He and my mother must have just had an argument! In any case, I liked the saying then because I could say "hell" and not get my mouth washed out with soap! It made me feel more like an adult to use such an ominous word. Naturally, I didn't have a clue as to what the saying meant.

I do now! As a pastor to single parents, I see the scorned all too often. Rejection is a terribly painful arrow. When you stick someone with it, you may create some first-class anger. No form of rejection begins to compare with divorce. It is industrial-strength rejection when compared with all others.

In divorce, the person who knows you best says you're not worth keeping anymore. Nothing causes more pain than that. The anger produced is a burning, seething type which can often become hatred. There are two typical ways people cope with this level of anger. You either "stuff it," which means you pretend that you are happy and doing just fine. Or, you can focus on it and seek revenge. Unfortunately, either way you lose. Stuffing leads to clinical depression. Hatred fills your life to the brim with a dismal, drab numbness. George Mac-Donald wrote, "Love makes everything lovely; hate concentrates everything on the one thing hated."

(The point is—if you are carrying this type of anger or hatred with you, it's sapping your strength away from your children, from your work and from anything worthwhile in your life.) And it is this kind of baggage, more than any other, that opens you up to the possibility of using any means, even your children, to gain revenge.

The answer is so easy we seem to trip over it. It is a single, simple word—*forgiveness.* We must forgive. If we don't, God's Word says He will not forgive us. The answer is complex, because we want the one who has hurt us to be hurt, too. We are not confident that God will be hard enough on whomever has hurt us so deeply. So, as in so many other matters, we help Him, suspecting that with all He has to do, He just might miss our particular situation.

This matter of forgiveness of former spouses is essential to healing. If you are struggling with it, turn to "The Servant As a Forgiver" in the Appendix and read what Chuck Swindoll has written on the subject. Many single parents in our church program have been greatly helped by this selection.

Depression

Depression is more or less unavoidable after a divorce or separation. I have now met thousands of divorced people and all of them have experienced some level of depression. How could they not? Their whole world has been turned upside down. It should make us feel better to know that the Bible has recorded many instances of depression in the lives of God's great saints. Moses became overwhelmed with the complaints and murmurings of the children of Israel. He asked God to take his life. You can't get much more depressed than that!

Elijah, the prophet, performed his greatest miracles on Mt. Carmel. The next thing we learn is that he, too, has fallen into a deep depression and is asking God to take his life

David was so depressed that he described himself as a worm and not a man.

Guess who else was deeply depressed. Jesus! Read Matthew 26:37,38:

> And taking with him Peter and the two sons of Zebedee, he began to be sorrowful and troubled. Then he said to them, "My soul is very sorrowful, even to death; remain here, and watch with me."

Being depressed certainly isn't a sin. But choosing to stay depressed for an unwarranted amount of time is. Depression is the proper response to a great trial. Climbing out of the pit of despair is appropriate also. Sometimes you may need professional help to relieve depression. If you need help, please seek it.

Not too long ago I counseled the mother of two high schoolers. Her husband had left her after 22 years of marriage and she was as depressed as any person I have ever met. She had lost several pounds and looked pale and weak. She told me that she cried for hours every night and was sleeping very little. Week followed week and I saw no progress. Her sorrow was so deep that, like Rachel mourning the loss of Joseph, she could not be comforted. She needed more help than I could give her.

I learned that her 14-year-old son was being deeply affected by her anguish. He often heard her weeping in the night, and sensed that he should not burden her with his own struggles. No one in the world was reaching out to his pain, and so he developed a way to gain attention.

He began stealing food from the school cafeteria for friends. They would pay him half of what it was worth and use the rest of their money for fun. He told me that he didn't know how to stop. When he tried, the kids he was stealing for threatened to turn him in to the school authorities. (I suspected he wanted to get caught anyway.) He asked me to pray with him so that he would find the courage to stop stealing. He was a Christian, and he knew it was wrong. He was weakened not only by his own difficulties, but also by his mother's.

I'm sharing this with you to encourage you to get help with your depression. That way your children will have a parent when they need one.

Do you want to feel better? There are several things you can do. No matter who you are, *you* must play the major role in your healing process.

1. Check your diet. Eating the right foods in the right amounts could dramatically improve your mood.

2. Exercise gives us all a feeling of accomplishment and releases endorphins into our systems. Endorphins are God's natural high and they make us all feel better.

3. Surround yourself with friends. Our pastor, Chuck Swindoll, once warned our single parents by saying, "Isolation is devastation, involvement is the answer." None of us can be happy in isolation for long. We just weren't made for it.

4. Make a short list of things you really want to accomplish. Then do them! It will give you a sense of achievement.

5. Whether you're a man or a woman, get some new clothes for yourself. And consider having your hair done differently. Feeling like a new person will affect your willingness to start over again.

6. Get a physical. Your depression may have physical causes that can be easily treated. If you're fine, then hearing your doctor say so will help you feel better.

7. Get back into regular study of God's Word. You can survive without it for a while, but not for long. It is from here that your hope

for the future comes. You are in the middle of a very dark chapter of your life. You need to know that your book has a happy ending! Read and reread Jeremiah 29:11: "For I know the plans I have for you, says the Lord, plans for welfare and not for evil, to give you a future and a hope."

8. Remember past times when things were bleak and got better. It helps to assure yourself that they will be better again. Just before David fought Goliath, he paused a moment to remember the times when he had killed lions and bears. Goliath didn't seem so big to David after his successful recollections.

Envy

I have yet to meet a single parent whose lifestyle didn't take a serious plunge after divorce. Two can definitely live more cheaply than one!

Experiencing a big drop in one's standard of living can be devastating. This is true because most of us measure success in financial terms rather than in terms of quality of life. When we see our possessions cut in half, it is easy to feel personally diminished.

It is also easy to fall into the trap of thinking we would feel better if we could be more financially independent. We would love to feel equal to our old friends, who seem to be able to buy what they need, travel where they want and enjoy recreation whenever they please. Such thinking is envy territory!

Envy means you resent your struggling situation and another person's successful one. Your life seems empty while other peoples' lives are full. Such feelings, fostered for any length of time, will probably lead to self-pity, anger and depression.

Now. Are you ready for this? If you have been feeling really terrible about being single, and you're envying married people, stop and remember. Did being married really make you happy? Face it. Being single isn't all bad! I asked my single parents one Sunday morning if they could see the good side of singlehood. Together we made a list.

- I can squeeze the toothpaste in the middle, back, front—anywhere on the tube I want!
- I don't have to explain why I am late and I am always late.
- I only have to make ½ of the bed.
- I no longer have to endure cold feet against my leg.
- I don't have to verify that the toilet seat is down before sitting.
- I can drink directly out of the milk carton.
- I don't have to go on a diet to support his efforts.
- I can run the air conditioner longer without being reminded what it costs.
- I can choose the TV station on Monday night.
- I don't have to pretend to like her parents anymore.
- I don't have to fold the towels in thirds anymore.
- I can belch after every meal.

I know too many single parents to say that singleness is easy. But it isn't all bad, either. And the key to being at peace is resolving to make the best of it without constantly envying those who have something different.

Paul wrote from a cold, dark, stinking jail, "I have learned, in whatever state I am, to be content" (Philippians 4:11).

Paul could say that because he had learned that Christ was his sufficiency. Christ was enough to satisfy his real needs. Paul didn't have everything he wanted. But he knew he had everything he needed.

The Scriptures take a hard-line on envy. It says in 1 Corinthians 13:4: "It [love] does not envy . . ." (NKJV).

James 3:16 is stronger yet: "For where envying and strife is, there is confusion and every evil work" (KJV).

In Galatians 5:21 it is made clear that those who spend their lives envying are among those who will not inherit the Kingdom of God.

It might be helpful to remember that the word "jealousy" and "envy" are interchangeable. It is also good to note that jealousy and envy are almost always linked with the word "strife." Envy sets you up to fight the person that you are envying. During and after a divorce, the person you are most likely to envy is your ex-spouse. It is easy to think that your ex has it better than you.

After five years of counseling, I observe that 85 percent of the divorces that come to my attention involve an affair. There is usually a third party in divorce situations, and for the one who is left behind, there is great pain. These individuals usually assume that their former mate is happy and fulfilled. Temporarily, that may be true, but it usually doesn't last. Only 5 percent of males marry the one with whom they've had the affair. If they do, the second marriage has less than a 24 percent chance of making it.

Envy and jealousy are a waste of time. If you will allow Him to, God will bring the necessary justice to your ex, and He will provide what you need. Psalm 68:5,6 is a great description of God:

> Father of the fatherless and protector of widows [the husbandless] is God in his holy habitation. God gives the desolate a home to dwell in; he leads out the prisoners to prosperity; but the rebellious dwell in a parched land.

Guilt and Shame

Two of the saddest loads carried by single parents are guilt and shame. Let's take a moment to distinguish between them. Guilt is the nagging feeling you have when you have sinned against God or someone else. True guilt is produced by a well-trained conscience or by the Holy Spirit. The feeling is designed to pull you away from the power of sin and to help you plead for God's forgiveness and the forgiveness of the person against whom you've sinned. Guilt is also designed to keep you from committing the sin again. It is a loud and clear signal that something needs to change and change quickly!

False guilt comes when you are involved in a failure and come to the incorrect conclusion that you were the cause. Sometimes this generates the faulty assumption that we are being punished for a sin when something terrible happens.

Shame is the proper response to true guilt. It is a sign of humility and true repentance.

The feelings that accompany guilt and shame are heavy, dark and gloomy. Unresolved, these feelings can devour us, rendering us useless. Confession is the answer, but don't confess until you're sure you understand what it is you have done. Then pray specifically, without compromise. Let me share several confessions that I've heard single parents pray:

1. Lord forgive me for committing adultery. I have disgraced Your name, destroyed my marriage and lost my way. Lord *help* me!

2. Lord Jesus, forgive me for what I did to my mate. He didn't deserve it. He was good to me. He doesn't want me back, Lord, because I drove him away. Forgive me Lord.

3. Lord forgive me. I can see the pain in my children's faces, Lord. It's too late for my

marriage, but help me help my children. It was my selfishness that did this to them. Heal them, Father. It wasn't their fault.

4. Lord, forgive me for knowing that I was doing the wrong thing and deciding to do it anyway. I shouldn't have thought, "When I am finished sinning God will forgive me." That cheapened Your grace. I'm sorry.

What do you do if you're experiencing false guilt, but you feel as though it is real? My advice is don't spend a whole lot of time trying to make that determination. Your belief that you are guilty is a powerful indictment, because Scripture clearly teaches that if you think something is sin, it is sin. Ask God's forgiveness and move on.

You may reeducate yourself later and have the added peace that you committed no offense. And by the way, don't spend any time trying to forgive yourself. What difference does that make? It is only God's forgiveness that matters. The feeling that we are still guilty comes from our lack of faith in God—we simply don't accept the fact that He has forgiven us.

Exhaustion

Exhaustion is the normal state of a single parent with primary physical custody. The reason is clear. Because parents love their children, they often try to pretend that life can continue just as before. So they sign up Kim for softball, Aaron for Little League, join the PTA, continue singing in the choir, volunteer for service organizations and work a full-time job at substandard wages.

For a while the illusion that life is "business as usual" persists. But then exhaustion rolls in like a June fog. Cooking one more meal, washing one more dish, cleaning up one more mess begins to feel like a climb up Mt.

Everest. Hands grow weak and shaky. Soon you're trying desperately to remember why you ever believed
parenthood to be a noble pursuit!

What you need is rest. By now, are you willing to
admit that you can't do it all alone? You weren't intended to, you know. You need a schedule adjustment
that will make your life manageable. Read on, because
in Chapter Six, you will find a special section on the
single-parent schedule. Be open to new ideas about
schedules and trust that there is a way!

Frustration

Your single-parent lifestyle is full of frustration. This
is to be expected, because you are taking on more than
any one person can possibly handle. Meanwhile, you are
not the only one influencing the lives of your children.
You will have to learn to accept the things you can't
change. And if you really cannot accept things as they
are, you will need to form an intelligent plan for change.

You're right. It is frustrating to have your child come
home stuffed with doughnuts and root beer. It's heartbreaking to know that your children are seeing your ex-
husband or ex-wife in the arms of another person. It's
maddening to hear that your six-year-old boy saw someone chain-sawed to death in an R-rated movie. It's
disturbing to hear that a stepparent slapped your child,
or banished him to his room for the weekend.

Frustration also comes from not enough money, not
enough time, not enough energy and not enough love
and affection. It may begin with a small, insignificant
incident, but it usually springs forth from deep, troubled
waters.

There are answers ahead for these frustrations, as
well as other equally perplexing problems. Take a deep
breath and remember—difficult as it is, single parenting is not an impossible task. And read on!

Economic Devastation

Let me reiterate: I have yet to meet a single parent whose economic outlook improved after a divorce. It's never easy to take a step downward—especially if the step takes you below poverty level. Are you struggling financially?

First of all, take time to meditate on the words of Jesus found in Matthew 6. Do you really believe His words? Do you really accept the truth that they apply to you?

> Therefore, I tell you, do not worry about your life, what you will eat or drink; or about your body, what you will wear. Is not life more important than food, and the body more important than clothes? (25).
>
> But seek first his kingdom and his righteousness, and all these things will be given to you as well. Therefore do not worry about tomorrow, for tomorrow will worry about itself. Each day has enough trouble of its own (33,34).

Whatever it is that worries you, just deal with today—so says our Lord. For more advice about financial specifics, turn to Chapter Seven. It could help you survive.

And if you're broke, don't feel alone. Believe me, you aren't!

Fears

When you have been emotionally injured through the death of a mate or a painful divorce you may experience fear of the future. You will wonder if you are destined to loneliness for the rest of your life. You will ask yourself, "Once someone else really gets to know me will he want to leave me too?"

If you have children, you will wonder how they will turn out without the benefit of two parents. At night you may feel vulnerable. You will ask yourself fearful questions: "How are my children doing without me?" "How can I start over again making new friends, building new relationships?" "How will I ever manage to go back to work?"

As you continue to read, you will find many of your fears being addressed in the pages to come. Facing your fears will put you in touch with reality. But, no matter what the circumstances, one principle remains true. God's Word is filled with the phrases "Fear not" and "Be not afraid." "Perfect love casts out fear," God's Word promises (see 1 John 4:18). God's love *is* perfect. And the better you know Him, the less afraid you will become.

Getting better acquainted with the loving God who deeply cares for you can set you free from your anxieties. Following His guidelines and principles for living will free you from your extra baggage. As you will soon see, He has had a lot of experience. He has been taking good care of single parents for several thousand years!

3

Father to the Fatherless

How well do you know Bible history? Can you name the first single mother? If you said "Hagar, maid to Abraham's wife Sarah," you were right. And the first single-parent child was Ishmael, Abraham's son by Hagar. Their story, in the Book of Genesis, also records the first divorce in Scripture. It is interesting to see how God handles it, and I think you will find the report encouraging.

Abraham and Sarah were married in Ur of the Chaldeans. This was located several hundred miles northeast of what we now know as Israel. One day Abraham received an unusual "call" to leave his home. He was instructed to go south to a land that would be given to his descendants forever.

Abraham's family had worshiped the Moon Goddess Nana, and his father was even named after her. But Abraham knew his call was from a far more powerful Being than the goddess. He felt compelled to go, even

though he and the Being had had no previous contact.
The Spirit of God must have assured Abraham that He
was very real indeed!

Abraham and his wife Sarah loved each other very
much, but they were unable to have children. In Abraham's day, that was ten times more tragic than it would
be now. It was a disgrace to Sarah, because barrenness
was always viewed as a curse from God. For Abraham, it
was devastating. He would be left with no heir, and he
was a very wealthy man.

God had promised Abraham and Sarah that they
would have a child—that Sarah's womb would be opened.
But, after giving His promise, He made them wait a
very long time, probably to test their faith. In the midst
of the wait, they became impatient. Both of them were
becoming too old to be parents, and they decided to help
God a little by devising a plan of their own. Sarah
dreamed it up and Abraham bought it.

Sarah suggested, since she was barren, that Abraham should have marital relations with her Egyptian
maid, Hagar. Since Hagar could own nothing, the offspring would, in essence, be Sarah and Abraham's baby.
In this way God's promise would be fulfilled.

So it was that Hagar became pregnant. Abraham was
delighted, but Sarah soon discovered that she had
opened a can of worms. Hagar became very proud that
she was carrying Abraham's child, and she started
treating Sarah with great contempt. She reminded
Sarah of her own barrenness and the poor woman was
soon beside herself with anger.

Bringing a third party into any relationship is not the
wisest thing to do, and Sarah, much too late, was faced
with her mistake. She accused Abraham of devising the
foolish scheme, and claimed it was his fault Hagar was
treating her this way. Abraham was stunned. "She's
your servant," he said, "so do with her what you please."
Well, it pleased Sarah to beat Hagar severely, so much so
that Hagar ran away and hid in the desert.

God was moved by Hagar's situation. She was no competition for the beautiful Sarah. Abraham would never see her as anything but a mistress—a vehicle for having children. She was born a slave and as long as she lived with Abraham, she would die serving a woman who hated the sight of her.

God has promised that He will be a Husband to the husbandless and a Father to the fatherless. The following passages illustrate very clearly how He does it. God is not just a husband and a father but a *good* husband, a *good* father.

> The angel of the Lord found Hagar near a spring in the desert; it was the spring that is beside the road to Shur (Genesis 16:7 NIV).

Notice that God went to Hagar. He didn't have to be asked.

> And he said, "Hagar, servant of Sarai, where have you come from, and where are you going?" (Genesis 16:8 NIV).

Gary Smalley has pointed out an interesting statistic. Studies reveal that men speak an average of 12,000 words a day, whereas women speak 25,000.[1] Gary didn't report that in order to make fun of women, but to show that God created them to be different than men. A good husband will appreciate his wife's need to share conversation, and he will talk with her. And so it is that God gives a little Egyptian maid the best chance she has ever had to communicate in-depth.

As a slave, she had been forced to say very few words. For one thing, her mistress didn't like her. For another, Sarah didn't consider anything she had to say to be very important. But the Lord asks her to tell Him her life's story.

The question, "Where have you been and where are you going," is open-ended. God gives her all the time in the world to explain, to remember and to tell Him her dreams for the future.

Hagar must have been touched by the Lord's willingness to listen. But in true slave fashion she keeps her comments brief and to the point. She says at the end of Genesis 16:8: "I'm running away from my mistress Sarai" (NIV).

The Lord stops and deals with that for a brief moment, giving her what must have seemed like bad news. "Go back to your mistress and submit to her" (Genesis 16:9 NIV).

The Lord always tells us what we need to hear, not what we want to hear. When you realize what would have been in store for Hagar if she had kept running, you will see that the Lord's request was reasonable. Pregnant Egyptian girls would have been in short supply in that part of the country and she would have been easy to find. She was carrying Abraham's child, so no stone would have been left unturned until she was located. Had she not returned by her own choice, she would have been punished severely.

And here is another factor. Even if she had escaped, her future would have included raising a fatherless child. Hagar's child would have surely been a slave. The Lord was speaking wisdom. She would always be a slave, but if she went back, there was a chance that her child would not. Her choices weren't the best, but the best choice was to go back. She would do it for the sake of the unborn child. She must have sighed a deep and sad sigh of resignation to her fate.

Then the Lord, sensing her despair, and her awareness of a bleak personal future quickly added, "I will so increase your descendants that they will be too numerous to count" (Genesis 16:10 NIV).

Now that was comforting. Someone would care for Hagar in her old age. There was dignity in a large family. That was just what Hagar needed to hear—

encouraging words. Suddenly life must not have seemed so bleak. God was speaking like a good husband convincing his wife that everything really was going to be okay.

Hagar had never been truly close to anyone, so it must have been quite a surprise when God revealed that He knew her intimately. Read Genesis 16:11:

> You are now with child and you will have a son. You shall name him Ishmael, for the Lord has heard of your misery (NIV).

Hearing she was pregnant was no big revelation, but learning that she was going to have a son was very extraordinary news. She knew Abraham would be pleased. A son was what he wanted more than anything!

But, even more touching to her, was God's compassion. She had never met anyone who knew her this well or cared about her personal misery. All at once, she was bathed in love. She must have wondered, "Why is this God even speaking to me? I've never given Him a second thought."

Hagar's gods were all Egyptian. What had they ever done for her? She had prayed to Ra, but he had never answered. Abraham's God was clearly superior. He cared for her. For the first time in her life, she felt as if she mattered to someone.

This kind and caring God even revealed to her what her son would be like. This wasn't the best disclosure that she was ever to hear, but at least it gave her the opportunity to be prepared.

> He will be a wild donkey of a man; his hand will be against everyone and everyone's hand against him, and he will live in hostility toward all his brothers (Genesis 16:12 NIV).

Well, it would be a while before he would become a man. Maybe, in the meantime, he would be a good little boy.

Hagar has the sweetest response to her conversation with the Lord. The Bible says, "She gave this name to the Lord who spoke to her: 'You are the God who sees me,' for she said, 'I have now seen the One who sees me'" (Genesis 16:13 NIV). Two things touched Hagar deeply. She was noticed and she was understood. The term, "who sees," means who understands. When we say "I see," we really mean "I understand."

"One who sees me" is Someone very special, very personal, indeed.

So now Hagar, an overlooked slave girl, was being listened to, cared about, blessed, made secure and completely understood by the God of the universe. And not only was she in His care, but her unborn son was, too.

I hope you are grasping the fact that these things apply to you, too. If you are like Hagar, without a mate and wondering about the future of your child or children, read the story gratefully. God never changes, and you can be sure that Hagar's blessings are yours as well.

The story does not end here. Hagar returns to Sarah, and months later gives birth to a healthy male child. As promised, Abraham names the child Ishmael. Abraham loves Ishmael, and for 13 years believes that Ishmael will be his heir—heir to the blessings of God. But that is not what God has planned. After a 13-year silence, God revisits Abraham and gives him some previews of coming attractions. We pick up the story in Genesis 17:15-18 (NIV):

> God also said to Abraham, "As for Sarai your wife, you are no longer to call her Sarai; her name will be Sarah. I will bless her and will surely give you a son by her. I will bless her so that she will be the mother of nations; kings of peoples will come from her."
> Abraham fell facedown; he laughed and said

to himself, "Will a son be born to a man a hundred years old? Will Sarah bear a child at the
age of ninety?" And Abraham said to God, "If
only Ishmael might live under your blessing!"

Abraham loves Ishmael so much that he is satisfied to
leave him his estate. He further asks if Ishmael might
receive the blessing of God. It is clear that Abraham
does not care whether Ishmael is Sarah's son. He sees
him as his firstborn. God says "Yes" to Abraham's
request, but it is not the yes that he expected.

Then God said, "Yes, but your wife Sarah
will bear you a son, and you will call him Isaac.
I will establish my covenant with him as an
everlasting covenant for his descendants after
him. And as for Ishmael, I have heard you: I
will surely bless him; I will make him fruitful
and will greatly increase his numbers. He will
be the father of twelve rulers, and I will make
him into a great nation. But my covenant I
will establish with Isaac, whom Sarah will
bear to you by this time next year." When he
had finished speaking with Abraham, God
went up from him (Genesis 17:19-22 NIV).

Just as promised, a year later Isaac was born to
Abraham and Sarah. Sarah nursed Isaac, and when he
was weaned (somewhere between one and two years
old), Abraham gave an enormous party to celebrate
Isaac's progress.

During the party, Sarah saw something she didn't
like at all. After talking to Abraham, Ishmael and
Hagar were sent away, but God still watched over them.

But Sarah saw that the son whom Hagar the
Egyptian had borne to Abraham was mocking, and
she said to Abraham, "Get rid of that slave woman

and her son, for that slave woman's son will never share in the inheritance with my son Isaac."

The matter distressed Abraham greatly because it concerned his son. But God said to him, "Do not be so distressed about the boy and your maidservant. Listen to whatever Sarah tells you, because it is through Isaac that your offspring will be reckoned. I will make the son of the maidservant into a nation also, because he is your offspring."

Early the next morning Abraham took some food and a skin of water and gave them to Hagar. He set them on her shoulders and then sent her off with the boy. She went on her way and wandered in the desert of Beersheba. When the water in the skin was gone, she put the boy under one of the bushes. Then she went off and sat down nearby, about a bowshot away, for she thought, "I cannot watch the boy die." And as she sat there nearby, she began to sob.

God heard the boy crying, and the angel of God called to Hagar from heaven and said to her, "What is the matter, Hagar? Do not be afraid; God has heard the boy crying as he lies there. Lift the boy up and take him by the hand, for I will make him into a great nation." Then God opened her eyes and she saw a well of water. So she went and filled the skin with water and gave the boy a drink.

God was with the boy as he grew up. He lived in the desert and became an archer. While he was living in the Desert of Paran, his mother got a wife for him from Egypt (Genesis 21:20 NIV).

As we will discuss in the chapters to come, all single-parent children will be damaged by their circumstances. They will never completely heal from the damage caused by divorce. That seems like a harsh statement, but the damage can be overcome in the same way a person can overcome or rise above any other handicap. Consider the facts concerning Ishmael, the son of Abraham.

God told Hagar that Ishmael would live in hostility with all of his brothers, and would be at war with them constantly. In other words, he would be filled with anger. It is not difficult, when considering the story, to see where his anger may have originated. When he was 15, almost 16, both he and his mother were divorced. Translated, that means "sent away." Nobody had prepared Ishmael for this. One day he was the firstborn son, heir to a fortune. The next day he was a homeless wanderer, without enough food and water to last a day.

Ishmael had watched Sarah degrade his mother, and he hadn't fared much better. Sarah had belittled him by refusing to call him Abraham's son. She only referred to him as "the slave's son." It must have been a wrenching experience to be sent away from a loving father with no warning and no explanation. It must have been horrifying to suddenly find himself, as well as his mother, facing a slow, painful death from thirst.

There is no record that Ishmael ever healed from this emotional trauma. He remained angry throughout the rest of his life. Yet, in spite this handicap, Ishmael became a great man through the blessing of God.

God's blessing to Ishmael had several aspects, as John Trent and Gary Smalley point out in their must-read book *The Blessing* (Thomas Nelson). God touched Ishmael, assured him of a wonderful future, gave him the skills that would insure his success, and stuck by him all the days of his youth. Genesis 21:20 is a very exciting verse for single parents—both mothers and fathers. It simply says, "God was with the boy as he grew up" (NIV). That's both quality and quantity time.

So why did Ishmael remain an angry person? God didn't force Ishmael to forgive his father or Sarah. I believe God would have dealt with him concerning the matter, but left the correct response up to Ishmael, just as he would with us.

In spite of his hostility, however, he apparently had a great life. Let's review it. First, he enjoyed the love and favor of Abraham for at least 15 years. Second, God took over the child-rearing responsibilities, so Ishmael moved from a good father to the best.

Hagar found a beautiful Egyptian wife for Ishmael. She gave birth to many children who eventually provided a multitude of grandchildren for Hagar. Ishmael became very wealthy, and 12 of his offspring became princes of their own kingdoms. The countries we now know as the Arab nations are the direct descendants of Abraham through Ishmael. Isaac's children were the inheritors of Israel and God's spiritual blessings. But Ishmael's offspring got all the oil. Today they're selling the oil on the world market at inflated prices and continue to buy more and more real estate. God is still blessing Ishmael's children to this day.

Do you see how God watched over Ishmael, and how Abraham's son rose above the hurts of his youth? In this same way God will be with your children. If they are willing, God will give them healing for their greatest hurts. With His help, only the scars will remain, just as the scars remained on the hands of Jesus.

God is indeed a Father to the fatherless. As with Ishmael, He will be there whenever He is needed, and will supply every necessity and much more. The fatherless child will be hurt, yes. But neglected? No. That's the way it was for Ishmael. That's the way it will be for your child. That's the way our Heavenly Father is and always will be.

God never changes!

4

A House Divided

Warning: The following chapter may be foreign to your present way of thinking!

Let's start with a few basic facts:

1. The single-parent home is still a family.

2. There is no reason in the world for a single-parent home to produce children destined for emotional illness or personal mediocrity.

3. Your children will reflect your personal values based on the way you demonstrate your beliefs.

So what am I getting at?

Sometimes moms and dads in my very special single-parents group ask me what I believe to be the greatest gift they can give to their children. I always give the same answer:

> Show respect to your former mate. And if there is any way in the world the two of you can work together cooperatively in the raising of your children—find it and do it.

Your response may sound something like this.

> Come on, Gary. Get real! If we couldn't work together for the children when we were married, why in the world are you suggesting we try to do it now that we are divorced?

To which I reply,

> Because it's the right thing to do. If you try and fail, at least your conscience will be clear. You will have acted in the best interests of your children. Most single parents don't act at all, or if they do, they act in their own best interests. If you do try and succeed, I guarantee that your children will be happier. They can't help but be.

Research clearly shows that, for some reason, children feel responsible for divorces. It takes very little imagination to see how they might get that impression. Put yourself in your child's little shoes and listen in on some past conversations. Do any of these words sound familiar?

1. If you really loved the kids you would spend more time with them and let them know you care.
2. I'm so tired of handling all the discipline I just want to scream.

3. He takes lousy care of the kids when he has them and it takes me a week to get them back into shape. All they eat are Twinkies and Big Macs. They're hyper for days.
4. I never have time for myself. All I ever do is take care of kid problems.
5. I don't know why he left. Ask him.
6. Don't ask me for new clothes. Your father's behind on the child support and I'm not made of money.
7. Listen, he left us, we didn't leave him.
8. He doesn't want to be with us anymore. He wants to be with her.
9. I figure if he can afford a new sports car he could buy you a pair of jogging shoes.
10. Who do you think loves you the most? I get stuck with all the day-to-day hard work, and your father takes you to Magic Mountain.
11. Listen, kids. I still want us to be a family. I never wanted a divorce—it was your mom's idea. She's the one that put you through this, not me.
12. I just wasn't happy. Things had to change or I was going to crack.
13. It's your weekend. I've made plans. Don't stick me with the kids. It's not my turn.

Children believe that the world revolves around them, and they interpret everything they hear into terms that they can understand. Now let's rewrite the list the way a child would hear it.

1. Somebody doesn't love me.
2. I'm a lot of trouble for everybody, and I'm making them crazy.
3. My daddy doesn't care enough to take good care of me.
4. I'm a problem.

5. Maybe I'm the reason Daddy left. Maybe that's why Mommy doesn't know.
6. Daddy doesn't care about my needs.
7. Daddy divorced me, too.
8. Daddy doesn't love me as much as he loves the new lady.
9. Daddy loves things more than me.
10. I have to choose who I love most, and it makes my mom feel bad.
11. Mom is the one who caused all this pain I'm feeling.
12. Mom's happiness is more important than my happiness.
13. I'm a problem and no one wants me.

Men can be just as verbally destructive as women, but they are with their children less than one-fourth of the time. Children generally don't hear the same tirades about Mom that they do about Dad. Sometimes men do, however, criticize their ex-wives too much in front of the children, leaving them forever caught in the middle.

In the midst of a recent custody battle, a child in our group told both of his parents that he wanted to live with them. Each one fought viciously to get him. When I talked to the boy, he admitted that he really wanted to go with his mom but didn't want to hurt his dad's feelings. When his father found that out, he graciously backed off.

I often recall the lyrics to a Karen Carpenter song: "Bless the beasts and the children, for in this world they have no choice, they have no voice." Children, and usually one mate or the other, didn't get a divorce—they *were* divorced.

For any of us, but particularly for a child, finding life to be out of control is a terrifying experience. Emotional upheaval goes on and on, and is devastating. Surely it is worth a prolonged effort to help your children develop respect for their other parent, even if that effort is personally very painful for you to deal with.

You can take your cues from a woman who lived two thousand years ago. It was clear that she felt that her child's needs were more important than her own. She was willing to go to any lengths, even so far as to be verbally abused, in order to meet those needs.

> Leaving that place, Jesus withdrew to the region of Tyre and Sidon. A Canaanite woman from that vicinity came to him, crying out, "Lord, Son of David, have mercy on me! My daughter is suffering terribly from demon-possession."
>
> Jesus did not answer a word. So his disciples came to him and urged him, "Send her away for she keeps crying out after us." He answered, "I was sent only to the lost sheep of Israel."
>
> The woman came and knelt before him. "Lord, help me!" she said.
>
> He replied, "It is not right to take the children's bread and toss it to their dogs."
>
> "Yes Lord," she said, "But even the dogs eat the crumbs that fall from their masters' table."
>
> Then Jesus answered, "Woman, you have great faith! Your request is granted." And her daughter was healed from that very hour (Matthew 15:21-28 NIV).

What made Jesus say that the woman's faith was great? There are four reasons. First, her faith *showed humility* because she was asking a Jew for a favor in a non-Jewish part of the country. The Jews and the Canaanites were longtime, sworn enemies.

Second, her faith *was persistent* in the face of resistance. At the outset, Jesus ignored her completely. Then He told her He couldn't do anything because helping Canaanites wasn't on His "to-do" list. His next response was to insult her race and her person with the term "dogs." Still, she just kept hanging in there.

Third, her faith was great because it *was unselfish.* Why was she putting up with all this? For her child. Her child's welfare was more important than her own.

Last, her faith was great because she knew her Jewish "enemy" was the only one who could help her, and *she believed in Jesus* despite His initial refusals. The stakes were high. A demon had her little girl, but there was a cure. Jesus had the antidote! She bowed before Him and begged. Jesus had the right to test her faith and He did. He will also test ours. I hope we pass!

In reaching out to your former mate, there is no assurance that he (or she) will cooperate. To tell you the truth, ex-spouses often don't. Eventually it will be up to them to go before God and explain their hatred, anger and unwillingness to help their children.

I can promise you two things with confidence: 1) If you try with a pure heart, God will be pleased and there will be a reward; and 2) if you try, there's a chance you may succeed. If you do, this will impact your children in a positive way for the rest of their lives. Nothing ventured, nothing gained.

If you attempt several times to work out a cooperative plan for the raising of your children, and your former mate simply will not respond, give it up, and try again in a year or two. Eventually you may realize that the idea is futile, and you will just have to develop a plan that excludes your ex. If that becomes the case, keep reading. The subject will be covered in a later chapter.

I want to make one matter perfectly clear—if your former spouse was physically abusive to you or your children—if she was alcoholic or drug dependent and could pose a threat to the children, if he is a sexual addict or mentally ill, you may as well turn to the next chapter.

If, however, you commit to trying for a co-op arrangement, let me suggest an approach. It's always good to go in with a plan. First, be prepared for an initial rejection. The first time you propose something, it may be resisted. Your ex may feel you want something from him, or that you are trying to be in control. You can understand those feelings, can't you? You might feel that way yourself, if the tables were turned.

Second, if he (or she) doesn't listen to your plan, suggest that he take a little time to think about it. There may be a necessary delay before you will be able to start working on it together.

Third, don't be under the illusion that all will go smoothly. Even if your effort only leads to some successes, it will all be worth it. Now let's talk about the plan that you might propose. Let's give it a title:

In the Best Interests of the Children

1. If you are both still single, agree to meet monthly to discuss the children's lives. Choose a neutral territory such as a restaurant as your meeting place. If your mate has remarried, make sure he's free to bring the stepparent. Stepparents play a major role in your children's development—a difficult role because they are rarely accepted by their stepchildren. Just don't allow your meetings to become a two-against-one situation. Whatever the equation, that would be totally unproductive.

2. Agree on a monthly agenda that, for the most part, deals only with the children.

3. Make a solemn vow never to demean one another. This is especially important when the children are present, or when you are in front of people who may see or talk to the children.

4. Make a list of decisions that are important for both of you to consider together.

5. Agree to defer to the gifts and knowledge of the other parent. Statements like, "You should ask your

mother that question. I don't know about those kinds of things," are very supportive. They will provide your children with the feeling that they are not being forced to take sides. They should not feel that they are in "enemy-occupied territory" when they are not with you.

6. Make sure you take time to share good news and interesting stories. Both of you are now missing blocks of time that can never be made up. It's important for you to fill in those blanks for each other.

7. Remind each other that raising children alone is not the way it was meant to be. When things get tense during your conversation, remember—sometimes they also get tense for those of us that are still doing it together! Hang in there.

Let's picture such a meeting and consider its benefits. Remember Bob and Susan Teal and their children, Charlyn and Jeff? Here's how things are going with them.

Eighteen months have passed—difficult months for everyone involved. Susan has given up her dream of Bob's return. His affair lingered for 11 months, and during that time, he and Susan bickered ceaselessly about the children.

Bob has also asked Susan to consider taking him back. After some consideration, she has declined. Susan feels she could never believe him again, and she could not remarry someone that she could not trust. She has received a promotion at work, and that has relieved some, although not all, of her financial pressure. She has joined a single-parent church group. Through that ministry, she has been able to forgive Bob for what he did to the family.

The forgiveness has given her freedom from the terrible feelings of anger she had previously experienced. Now she can actually say that she hopes someday he'll be happy. She isn't sure if she's happy herself, but she has a clear conscience and has finally adjusted to the single-parent lifestyle.

Today Susan can say with confidence that she doesn't find singleness all bad. Several close friends and a support group have helped her deal with her difficulties and with the problems of her children. She has even begun to date again, with the understanding that she will take it very slowly for fear of being hurt.

Bob has broken things off with Ginger and is, for the most part, a very lonely man. He has absorbed himself in his work and has a very limited social life. The highlight of his life is seeing his son Jeff.

Jeff is doing much better. His grades are up again, and he is no longer a behavior problem at school. Jeff enjoys being with his father and at times even wishes that he could live with him.

Charlyn has just completed a drug rehabilitation program which she entered by her own choice. Much of her better self has returned and she is even willing to see her father on a somewhat regular basis. She won't stay with him on weekends, but is willing to go out to dinner once a week and talk. She has even come to the place where her dad can tease her again. This has happened since Bob wisely wrote a letter asking her to forgive him. In the letter he took full responsibility for the pain he brought upon his family.

In some ways that letter marked the beginning of Charlyn's healing process. Her counselor had once cautioned her that her healing would never be complete until she was able to forgive and relate to her father in some sensible way.

Recently, Susan's pastor has recommended that the single parents in his group should make greater efforts to cooperate with their ex-spouses in child raising. Upon hearing this suggestion, Susan felt sure that such an effort might work for her and Bob. And so she has contacted him and asked if they could meet at a restaurant to talk the idea over.

The night has arrived. When she first called, Bob had no idea what Susan meant by "cooperating." He felt a little defensive. He was afraid that he was going to be blamed for something-or-other the children were doing wrong.

Susan begins, "Bob, last Sunday our pastor pointed out that it was best for our children if you and I could work together to raise them. We are both missing out on some of the best times of their lives, and they are going to be facing some bad days, too. Maybe we can share in all of it. As hard as I try, I haven't been able to be everything the children need when they are with me. The pastor said it would be best for us to first talk about where we need help."

So far, Bob doesn't hear anything unreasonable. "How did the pastor say that we should work together?" he asks. "I mean, is there a formula or agenda or something to follow?"

"Well, yes" Susan says. "There are some basic rules. We should agree to meet monthly—away from the children, in case we get into an argument. We have to decide what we need to talk about. That means setting an agenda. The agenda should deal only with the children so we're not tempted to interfere with each other's lives. We have to make a solemn promise to never say anything bad about each other so that the children are never forced to take sides. We never want to make them feel that they have to love one of us more than the other."

Bob scratches his chin and says, "Can you give me an example of something we might want to talk about?"

"Well, yes, I can, as a matter-of-fact," Susan begins. "Last Friday Jeff was very angry with me because I wouldn't let him see an R-rated movie with his buddy's family. It was a horror movie. I had read the reviews in the newspaper. It was plotless—one of those movies where kids at a summer camp are chain-sawed, stabbed, strangled and shot to death. You know how I love those kinds of films, right?"

"Oh, I get it," Bob snaps. "This is about what kind of movies I should take Jeff to, isn't it?"

"No! It isn't that at all! Please hear me out. I know it isn't my business to tell you what you should or shouldn't do when you're with Jeff. I understand that, and I know you've respected my time with Jeff. I appreciate that very much. The problem is a bit different than that. You see, Jeff threw a tantrum when I told him he couldn't go to see *Chain-Saw Massacre* with his friend. He kicked the wallboard and put a sizable hole in it, right by the front door."

"You've got to be kidding!" Bob is horrified.

"I wish I were. I grounded him for the evening, and then, to make matters worse, he used some pretty strong language to let me know how he felt about it. You picked him up the next morning. When he got home on Sunday afternoon he taunted me with the fact that you took him and his friend to see *Chain-Saw Massacre*. It was one of those times when I felt all alone because Jeff had figured out a way to take authority out of my hands. Bob, I need your help."

Bob still co-owns the house with Susan. His first question is, "Did you have the hole fixed yet?"

Susan says no, and Bob offers to do the repair job.

"Bob, how would you like me to handle these kinds of situations? Do you want to know about them?"

"Well, part of me wants to say yes and the other part wants to say no. I know Jeff shouldn't get away with these kinds of things, but when I only get to see him every two weeks, I hate to get stuck punishing him every time I see him. But I guess I hate the thought of raising a brat even more. What do you think?"

"Well, I'll tell you what I've been thinking. I was hoping maybe you and I could have a brief chat on the phone before you come to pick him up. Of course it wouldn't be fair to ask you to carry out some horrendous punishment at the last minute every week. But maybe if we work together, neither of us will have it quite as hard."

Susan smiles before she continues. "I think he's become quite an operator. He's driving me crazy, and in the meantime he's hitting you up for a bundle every other weekend. You're taking him to shows, out to eat and he's coming home with gifts. There must be a better way for both of us!"

Bob looks out the restaurant window and says, "I hate the Disneyland Dad role. I really do. But I'm so afraid Jeff won't want to see me unless I make elaborate plans. There are lots of Saturdays when I'd just like to relax, watch college football, play catch or walk and talk. But it doesn't seem special enough. He's old enough to choose what he wants and he might not want me. And that scares me to death. You're right about him costing me a fortune. We spend a bundle when he's here."

"So what should we do?"

"Susan, what if I tell Jeff we'll be doing something special *if* I get a good report when you and I talk. It might be good for him to know that we're working things out together."

"I'm pretty sure my punishments would have more clout if he knew that. He's supposed to be weeding the backyard as a penalty for making the hole in the wall. But he hasn't gotten very far."

"Susan this wallboard thing really bugs me. I'll talk to Jeff and let him know that he and I won't be doing *anything* 'fun' until the hole is fixed *and* the weeds are pulled."

"Thank you Bob, I'd really appreciate that. But isn't there anything you want to talk about? You've been kind enough to hear me out."

Bob is silent, not sure how to word his question. "I don't know if you can help me or not, Susan. Things are so different with Charlyn. She's willing to see me now, but when we go out to dinner we don't talk about anything important. I don't know what to say to her. And most of the time I'm afraid to say anything for fear I'll make her mad at me again. Can you help me find my way back to my little girl? How does she really feel about me? Does she have a boyfriend? I guess I'm just asking for anything you can give me, even though I know this is my own fault."

Susan is surprised to see Bob revealing any pain. This is the first time he has accepted any blame for the children's difficulties. She figures it's time he knew what has happened in Charlyn's life during the last year and a half. If only someone else were there to tell him!

Choosing her words carefully, Susan starts to recount the sad tale. "Bob, I don't know where to begin. It's been a long 18 months for Charlyn. Most of what I'm going to tell you, she wouldn't want you to know. No matter what she has said or how she has acted, she loves you very much and someday I believe you will have a terrific relationship."

"I sure hope so." He shakes his head.

"Bob, she was just released from a drug rehabilitation program about five weeks ago. Prior to that, she went into a deep depression and began talking about suicide. Her best friend told me about it and I insisted that she go and see a professional counselor. The counselor was very good with Charlyn and a lot came out in a little time. It seems—well, Bob, she was hooked on cocaine and was financing her habit with sexual favors."

"Oh, no, Susan!"

"It seems a drug dealer on her campus was taking advantage of her and, if it will keep you from killing him, you'll be glad to know that he's in jail. I turned him in."

Bob is in shock, overcome with waves of guilt, anger and confusion. "Why am I just now finding this out?"

"Bob, I wanted to tell you and truly felt that you should know, but Charlyn was too ashamed. She asked me not to. Her counselor advised me to wait. She felt that Charlyn needed to be free of the drugs before she could begin to deal with her relationship with you. I did the best I could with the advice I was given and I'm sorry that you were left out. I know that hurts you. But for what it is worth, it was Charlyn's counselor that talked her into letting you back into her life."

Bob bows his head and asks, "Did the counselor ever explain to you why Charlyn did what she did?"

"I wish you hadn't asked that question, Bob. Please don't hate me for telling you. Are you sure you wouldn't rather ask the counselor yourself?"

"No, I'd rather you tell me. I know you're in a rough spot, but I want to know."

"Okay, here goes. It seems that Charlyn was at that tender age of change at about the time you left. She was withdrawing from me so that she could grow up. Apparently, during that period, she was reaching out to you. She was even competing with me for your attention and approval. When you moved out, she felt like you were divorcing her as well as me. She became very angry. Whenever she thought of you with Ginger and Amber, her anger grew and grew until she felt intense pain. She couldn't stand the pain so she turned to drugs to feel better."

Susan pauses, allowing Bob to absorb her words.

"She needed male approval and the feeling of being connected. Because of this, she became very available to boys. Anyway, she's doing much better now and the fact that she wants to be with you is a very good sign. I know that you didn't mean for any of this to happen. I know you are feeling guilty. I did too."

"What on earth did you feel guilty about?" Bob asks in amazement.

"Oh, I felt that if I had been a better wife none of this would have happened."

Bob sits speechless, large tears forming in the corners of his eyes. "It wasn't your fault, Susan," he says quietly.

"I know," Susan says, as lightheartedly as possible. "Look, I'm not worried anymore about who's to blame. I'm in a healing process and I have to leave the past behind. Anyway, Bob, I think our meeting went pretty well. Don't you?" She squeezes Bob's hand and they smile at each other. "We can't afford to spend any time being guilty or angry. We have two wonderful children to raise and we really need each other. I don't know if I have ever said it, but I want you to know you're forgiven."

In case you're wondering, your meetings aren't likely to go as well as Bob and Susan's. I'll bet you and I could make a list of 20 reasons why this kind of arrangement would never work in your situation. But you will never know if you don't try!

The worst that can happen is the rejection of your ex-mate. But haven't you handled that before? Let the Canaanite woman set an example for you. Are you acting unselfishly on behalf of your children? Are you humble enough to deal with the "enemy" because he is the best source of help you have? Are you persistent in your pursuit of the children's good? Do you believe in God's power to provide help?

If so, you are demonstrating great faith. God will be pleased. And with Him working alongside you, you will never feel so alone again. He will always be there, whether you are left to work things out on your own or whether you aren't.

5

When There's No One Else

Are you one of the many single parents who do not have the option of dealing with another responsible party? Is the job of raising the children yours and yours alone?

Widows and widowers suddenly find themselves being mothers and fathers through no choice of their own. They never dreamed it would happen to them. They must care for their children while still grieving the loss of a mate who can't return to help them.

Other men and women become single parents when lovers take off and refuse to share the responsibility for their offspring. These individuals feel abandoned, not knowing where the other parent has gone, and wondering whether he (or she) is even alive. In some ways the saddest group of single parents are those who live across town from former mates or lovers who have been abusive, or are heavy users of drugs or alcohol. None of these situations is easy to bear, but there is a way. It is called Plan "B."

Plan "B" begins with a reminder—God is a Father to the fatherless. Women, remember Hagar. God is also a Husband to the husbandless, so you are not alone. Men, the Word of God promises that He will be your sufficiency and your portion. You have not been abandoned, either.

When you are lacking any good thing, you have the right as a child of the King to ask for it. The practical solution for your problem begins (but doesn't end!) when you ask the Lord for help. Read Luke 18:1-8 (NIV):

> Then Jesus told his disciples a parable to show them that they should always pray and not give up. He said: "In a certain town there was a judge who neither feared God nor cared about men. And there was a widow in that town who kept coming to him with the plea, 'Grant me justice against my adversary.'
>
> "For some time he refused. But finally he said to himself, 'Even though I don't fear God or care about men, yet because this widow keeps bothering me, I will see that she gets justice, so that she won't eventually wear me out with her coming!' "
>
> And the Lord said, "Listen to what the unjust judge says. And will not God bring about justice for his chosen ones, who cry out to him day and night? Will he keep putting them off? I tell you, he will see that they get justice, and quickly. However, when the Son of Man comes, will he find faith on the earth?"

As I said, every practical solution begins with prayer. In this case, the prayer should be, "Help me Lord to meet the needs of my children. I am not enough." Once you have asked, be ready to accept the help He sends. But keep it in mind that He expects you to be wise and do your part.

Our human nature may implore us not to ask for help. In humility we must be willing to go against that tendency and ask anyway. What should you ask for? You can make a list of your own needs, but I can guess some of them.

Single Parent Needs

1. Emotional support
2. Practical help (car maintenance, balancing the checkbook, fixing the garbage disposal, etc.)
3. Rest
4. Babysitting
5. Money
6. Help with the child discipline
7. Adult conversation
8. Counsel for major decisions
9. Guidance on future relationships
10. Someone to "play" with (yes, you need to play)
11. Someone to cry with
12. A good listener
13. A good role model of the opposite sex for your children
14. Help reentering the job market
15. Someone to hold you and assure you that you and your children are going to be all right

You and I both know the list could go on and on. All of us have quantities of needs, and those of us who have been wounded have a good many more. The list itself may have caused you to feel desperate—for the moment you can't imagine how any of your needs will be met. Well, don't despair! Help is all around.

The Four Basic Help Groups

Just as there are four basic food groups, there are four basic help groups:

- Family
- Friends
- Church
- Government agencies

Family

Your family should be able to help you meet many of your needs. Even dysfunctional families can provide help, love and concern. But before I proceed, I'll have to ask you a personal question. What kind of family relationship did you have before you became a single parent and your needs increased? If your relationships were unhealthy, then you may need to do some fence-mending before making any requests. If apologies are in order, make them.

Your parents and siblings are human. They may not be all that glad to help you out if your relationships have been marred with tension. Nevertheless, the Bible commands us to ask, so we can assume it is appropriate. But how we ask, when we ask and why we ask will certainly have a bearing on whether or not we receive!

The prodigal son provides a model for us. When he left home, he didn't leave on good terms. He had requested a third of everything his father owned. For whatever his father's own private reasons may have been, his request was granted. The son ran away, wasted all his resources, and found himself in a desperate plight.

When he came to his senses, he said, "How many of my father's hired men have food to spare, and here I am starving to death! I will set out and go back to my father and say to him: Father, I have sinned against heaven and against you. I am no longer worthy to be called your son; make me like one of your hired men." So he got up and went to his father.

But while he was still a long way off, his father saw him and was filled with compassion for him; he ran to his son, threw his arms around him and kissed him. The son said to him, "Father, I have sinned against heaven and against you. I am no longer worthy to be called your son." But the father said to his servants, "Quick! Bring the best robe and put it on him. Put a ring on his finger and sandals on his feet. Bring the fattened calf and kill it. Let's have a feast and celebrate (Luke 15:17-24 NIV).

Maybe you have nothing for which to repent. No matter. A humble attitude is always an appropriate posture when you are in need. It will invariably bring forth greater blessings. Many of you don't need that reminder. Your spirits are already broken.

Whatever your state of mind, by all means ask, being thankful for whatever your family can do. Just don't be angry about what they *won't* do. God may want to provide for you in other ways, and from other places. He must always be allowed to choose your means of rescue. And let me say that all your help will probably never come from one source. If it does, that source will come to own you.

If you do choose family help, especially from parents, bear in mind that parents will usually act like parents, clinging a bit to the control they had when you were younger. Don't resent it—they can't help it! Parents feel older and wiser. Besides, it is their time and resources you are using, which gives them some right to express their opinions. Hopefully, they will always be kind and wise, but don't count on it. And, if your parents or family don't help at all, don't hate them for it. Just expect help to come from somewhere else. It will!

Friends

I hope you have friends. If you do, they can meet some of your most overwhelming needs. They can encourage you spiritually and emotionally. They can provide a restful harbor from life's storms. They can feel your heartbeat. Friends can provide the best nonjudgmental conversation. If they are wise and knowledgeable, they can help you make important decisions. Friends can point out flaws in relationships and observe problems which we might otherwise overlook.

You can play with friends and share babysitting with them. Friends can provide role models for your children and they can assure you everything is going to be all right. Just don't borrow money from them! Mark Twain once described friendship as "that enduring institution that will withstand anything if not asked to lend money."

The single-parent lifestyle can be rather financially spare. If you borrow money you may find it very hard to pay it back, even though repayment was your most sincere intention. And while you are worrying about the troublesome matter of reimbursement, you will feel awkward in your friend's presence. The truth of the matter is, you need the wealth of benefits that friendship brings far more than you need money.

If a friend offers to lend you money, explain that there is too much chance that you won't be able to pay it back. If your friend offers a financial gift, take it—if there are no strings attached. It may well be God's way of meeting your needs. The Lord taught, "Owe no one anything, except to love one another; for he who loves his neighbor has fulfilled the law" (Romans 13:8). When things are better for you in the future, and you are able, you may want to pass the gift on, in love, to someone else.

The Church

Until recently the Christian Church has failed to reach out to single parents. I believe the neglect of this needy group of people has come about for all the wrong reasons. For one thing, churches have been too proud to admit that they haven't been able to stem society's tide of divorce and immorality. Single parents are hard, clear evidence of the Church's failure to make families strong and to provide reason and accountability for moral behavior.

Another problem is that single parents and their children have a deep well of needs. Up to now, the Church has preferred building programs and other less taxing ministries. Frankly, most pastors don't know what to do with the complex and never-ending problems faced by single parents. And they don't have time in their already busy schedules to find out. But things are changing.

There is now a generation of elder churchmen and churchwomen who have seen their own children's marriages crumble. They have softened their hard positions on touchy marital issues. They are now willing to find innovative ways to help.

The Church has always moved slowly, but it usually makes solid, wise progress when it does.

Thirteen years ago our church began to reach out to single parents. The first night they met, 40 single parents and 12 volunteers came into contact with each other. Healing began to occur. What started as a weeknight support group soon expanded. Before long, weekly socials for adults and their children were added. A Sunday school class and a divorce recovery program followed.

After developing a program for wounded adults, a similar project was pioneered for children who had been injured by the divorce process. A critically high failure rate in second marriages also led the single-parent fellowship to research and create a program to prepare people for remarriage.

Our Singles Fellowship is currently touching the lives of 700 different people each month, and it is still growing. Senior Pastor Chuck Swindoll is one of the group's biggest cheerleaders. Our congregation is proud of the responsible and godly way our single parents serve their church.

I was hired five years ago as the first full-time single parents' pastor. Today I'm hearing from churches all over the United States who are begging for help as they pioneer similar ministries. The Christian Church is finally waking up to the need. They are, as Dietrich Bonhoeffer would say, "coming out into the tempest of living."

If you are a single parent and live anywhere near a large city, a single-parent program probably exists within your locality. It can help you in ways that you can't imagine, so take the time to find it. Make sure the group's primary focus is on the Lord Jesus Christ and that His Word is believed without apology. Be concerned if there is not a healthy balance between Christian psychology and Scripture. When the two disciplines are in conflict, side with the Word of God. Psychology is a young and sometimes helpful field, but it is in no position to debate or replace a strong and personal faith.

A church single-parents program shouldn't be primarily a social group, important as fellowship is. It's first function should be to draw you and the others closer to Christ. When that happens there will be laughter, tears, healing and then the ability to move on with your life.

If your church is too small to have a single-parent program, that doesn't mean the church leaders don't care. And it doesn't mean you should quit, either. Three out of 5 of our single parents attend other churches, and nearly 20 percent are from a Catholic background. They all contribute wonderful perspectives to all that we do.

What help can you realistically expect from your church?
Your church should be able to help you, in a limited way, get through emergencies. Their benevolence fund may enable you to fix your car, pay your electric bill, or provide necessary school clothes for your children. Some churches have a food fund which can assist with the reduction of monthly food costs. Most churches provide financial assistance for needy people, and they may be glad to help you. But you will probably have to ask. Only the most sensitive individuals will notice your dilemma and seek you out.

Your pastor ought to be able to encourage you, assuring you that God is present and on your side despite your difficulties. He should be spiritually and emotionally equipped to guide you through the emotional trauma of a divorce. Most ministers have had some training in counseling, and should recognize whether your needs exceed their abilities. A wise pastor is worth his weight in gold, and his advice won't cost you anything. The price is right!

If possible, go through the valley of divorce with family, friends and a wise pastor rather than an expensive professional counselor. It is likely that the only thing a professional will have to offer that the other people don't is a big bill. Save talented professional counselors for deep needs and for abnormal circumstances. What you're looking for is free. It can be found within a deep faith in Christ, in family and in close friends.

Government Agencies

Government Agencies can be of great assistance and can provide long-term solutions. They can help with low-cost housing, food, medical aid, job training and education. All of us—you, your friends and your family members—have been paying into these programs for years. There is certainly no shame in taking advantage of them.

Thank God that we live in a country that makes provision for hard times, even though most government aid provides only a subsistence level of support. The help you need is all around you but you may have to do a little detective work to find it. I suggest you call the largest churches in your town or area. Usually, there is an assistant pastor who handles counseling at large churches. He keeps informed of the community services. As a matter-of-fact, his secretary is usually even more informed. Begin by calling your church or any large church.

The Yellow Pages and the public library are also a great source of help. Don't be afraid to ask the librarian for help.

In Orange County, California, where I work, Glenda Riddick published a book entitled *Resource Directory for Orange County*. It has more than 4000 places to contact for service and assistance. Don't be afraid to contact your local city hall for local service referrals. You will be surprised to find out how many people want to help!

I can tell you this with confidence—you are not alone in the care and raising of your children. There are many who will stand with you. You may find yourself living well below the standard to which you've become accustomed, but that's okay. Your needs will be met. Tell yourself, over and over, "I am in a difficult chapter of my own autobiography. This chapter will end. The best days for me, and my children, are yet to come."

The Noncustodial Parent

Feeling alone in the care of children can take many forms. Being the primary caretaker is certainly a solitary job. Being the only caretaker is a monumental task. But there is immense loneliness in the prospect of having only occasional opportunities to see your own children. Nobody wants to be a part-time parent.

Custody battles almost double the cost of divorce, yet both parents are willing to pay dearly rather than lose precious time with their beloved children. Ninety-seven percent of the time the father is assigned the part-time role. And, in most cases, that is what is best for the children. It isn't that Mom is more important than Dad when it comes to child development. She clearly isn't. Both parents are important for different reasons and at different times. It's just that mothers are usually slightly better-prepared culturally for the practical responsibilities, while fathers are better prepared to pay child support because of inequities in our salary system.

Still, being the noncustodial parent is not an easy fate for a loving parent. One of my closest friends, Jake, fought a bitter battle to gain custody of his son and daughter. He won the first round in court, but his wife appealed and won the second judgment.

Jake could see that it was going to be a never-ending battle so he decided not to appeal and reluctantly accepted the role of part-time dad. How he hated it! He often confided his frustrations to my wife Carol and me. I wrote a song to work out my burden over what I saw happening to Jake. Here's a portion of it:

Part-Time Dad

Happy times the memories fading,
Children's laughter has gone astray.
Locked alone in life's dark shading,
Longing for a sunshiny day.
Gray the dawn, my life is silent.
Gone the dreams for which I've paid.
Mind is spinning, spirit's joy spent,
Nursing wounds this strife has made.

Saturday, here come the children,
Growing tall and looking grand.
Do you want some chocolate candy?
Want to go to Disneyland?
Does your mother still embrace you?
Does the new man tuck you in?
Read you stories, get you Band-Aids?
Gee, I've missed you, how you been?

Breaking bonds that God has joined forever.
Killing love He'd given by His grace.
The children cry, they feel the pain forever,
Touching scars time never will erase.

Rich, another one of our close friends, lost his wife to his best friend. His feelings of betrayal produced rage that burned for years. Rich finally decided that these feelings were devouring him. He realized that he must have a forgiving heart or live in agony.

Several years later, his former best friend wrote him a letter asking for forgiveness. Rich wrote him back a marvelous letter that captures the anguish a noncustodial parent goes through. I quote from it, in part:

> Brad, your letter has caused me to reflect on the past ten years. The two things that stand out most are the loss of my boys and being betrayed. The times that you now take for granted with my sons are moments that were mine. The good, the bad, the happy, and the sad are all times that should have been mine. I'll never retrieve that time and neither will my sons...."

In some ways these two documents, the song and the letter, sum up the dilemma and pain of part-time parents. Think about the different problems they face.

1. They feel obligated to lavishly entertain their children during weekend visits. Their

fear is that their children need an incentive or they won't want to see them.

2. They miss most of the meaningful moments of their children's lives. They get everything secondhand, after it has already happened.

3. They watch other people begin to fulfill the roles they once played in their children's lives.

4. They watch their children hurting and failing but are not there to help them heal or succeed.

5. Often they are not consulted on important decisions that affect the future of their children. They feel helpless.

6. As the children grow, they realize that weekend visits are more and more a drag. Their kids want to be with their friends or just stay home and relax.

Nothing will ever change the fact that you are the parent—you always will be. If your separation from your children was your fault, you will just have to face up to that. It may be that you will never gain access to your children's hearts until you ask their forgiveness. If they see you as guilty, they will be loyal to the injured party. They will feel obligated to punish you for your part in the divorce or separation.

Many children feel like *they* have been divorced. I have listened carefully, and rarely do I hear children say, "Daddy left Mommy." They usually say, "My Daddy left us," or "Daddy left the family." Try to be sensitive to what you hear them say and to what they think. Don't make the serious mistake of assuming, "They'll get over this in a while." They don't completely get over it at all. They simply find the strength to face it. You will have to help them, and they will also never outgrow their need for your assistance.

Now, let's consider several ways in which you can be the best part-time parent possible. I'm going to share what I've learned from the most outstanding of my part-time dads.

1. *Let your children know where they can reach you at all times.* Encourage them to call you anytime, night or day, if they need to. They may never call, but I can assure you that the access you are giving them means a lot.

2. *Between visits, call your children once or twice a week, or even more frequently if they are very young.* Be sure to say, "I love you," and use their names when you do. Try to be thoughtful about their schedules, taking into consideration your former spouse's needs as well. For example, are you interrupting your children's favorite TV program? Is it dinnertime? Or after bedtime? Keep the phone calls short, and find out whether they are causing any emotional pain.

3. *Children love mail. A "thinking of you" card with a short note will always be treasured.* If your children have special interests, include magazine articles, newspaper clippings or cartoons that connect with their interests. It tells them that you have been thinking about them when you aren't around. That means a lot.

Tell them about special, interesting things that have happened to you. Stay away from messages that would make them feel guilty or sad.

Saying things like "I would love to hug you and kiss you but you aren't here," will hurt and frustrate your child. "I'll look forward to seeing you a week from Friday, with love Dad," will do just fine. Below is a sample letter to a 10-year-old son,

> Dear Tad,
> I remembered that you were doing a report on dinosaurs and saw this magazine article. I thought you might be able to use it. Great

pictures, huh? I liked dinosaurs a lot when I was your age. I'll bet your report is going to be super. I'm proud of how you're doing in school and would be happy to help you do any homework when you stay with me on the weekends. I always love being with you, not only because you're my son but because you're my buddy, too.

I got a bonus at work and I'm going to get a new TV for the apartment. I'm going to wait till next week so you can help me pick it up at the store.

And guess what Tad? I'm going to teach you how to paint a house! Grandma's house needs painting and I said you and I would help her. Maybe you can earn enough to take us to the movies on Saturday night. I know you've been wanting to see the latest *Star Trek* and it sounds great for guys your age. See you Friday at 6:00 P.M. sharp.

Love, Dad

4. *If possible, before you pick up your children, ask your ex if there is anything you should know about—health, discipline, accomplishments, disappointments, heartbreaks.* This will enable you to be sensitive, and to enter into their lives in a way that really makes a contribution. Get away from the idea that these visits are only for the purpose of meeting your own emotional need to be near to your children. Instead, keep asking, "What can I do to make my children's lives better?"

5. *Don't give in to the temptation to avoid discipline.* It is natural to feel that your children won't want to be with you if you correct them for doing something wrong. But nothing could be further from the truth. They won't respect you if they are *not* disciplined.

6. *There are some things that should never occur when the children come to visit.* Let's make a list of those things, remembering that they are in the best interests of the children.

A. The children should never hear you say anything disrespectful about your former mate. Such talk puts children in a terrible position. If they agree with you, they will have dishonored one of their parents and broken one of God's commandments. If they don't, they will have offended you. Most certainly, you will find yourself standing before God one day explaining why you caused them to stumble.

B. Never use your children as a "news service" to find out what the ex-spouse is doing. That's my extra-nice way of saying "Don't force your children to be spies!" Boys and girls were not designed for that role, and worse yet, you are likely to turn them into liars. They will tell you what you want to hear in order to survive in your presence. Then they will turn around and tell their mom (or dad) what they believe she (or he) wants to hear. Single-parent children often learn to do this in order to survive.

C. Don't take your children to R-rated movies. That is generally the best policy. The only exception would occur when you have discussed the possibility with your former spouse, and the two of you have agreed that the value of the film in question is sufficient to merit an exception. Older children would, for instance, profit from seeing and discussing a film such as *Rainman*. This movie demonstrates excellent values, although it does feature some rather rough language. (Probably no rougher than what kids hear at any public junior high school in the country, however!)

Consider the pressure your children experience when they are raised under two sets of values. It is very confusing to them, and they are faced with the task of either defending your choices or lying to the other parent about how they spent their weekend.

D. Try to agree with your former spouse on an estimated bedtime. When, week after week, you bring the children home exhausted, you won't find your ex an enthusiastic supporter of your visitation times. And chances are, if you received weary, cranky children on a regular basis, you would be annoyed too. Late bedtimes should be the exception and not the rule.

E. Try to feed the children food that is worth eating. McDonald's, Jack in the Box, Wendy's and Burger King are *not* the four basic food groups! They provide overly processed and highly refined foods which contain far too much sugar. Bringing home a carload of children filled with fast-food is like dropping off a litter of pit bulls!

F. Never allow an ugly scene to ruin the children's return home. If there is a problem, tell your former spouse that you will call to discuss it later. Then leave quickly. It is unbelievably painful for the children to hear your angry voices.

7. *Avoid the weekend spending trap.* This is for the children's good, as well as for yours. Use your weekends

to help other people. Visit relatives. Now and then include friends they run around with at school. Build or fix things. Show them what you do at work. Prepare a meal together. Read them a book and leave off at a suspenseful place, making the children wait for the next visit to see what happens. Above all, talk about important things without giving too much advice they don't ask for.

8. *Hug them and tell them you love them often.* Pats on the back, hugs and squeezes are needed also. Any appropriate physical contact, including roughhousing, is very much in order.

9. *Choose a hobby that you would like to pursue together.* This is an excellent hook to keep them wanting to see you.

Face the facts—the day may come when your children may not want to see you as frequently. If you have done your homework, and given them your best efforts at noncustodial parenting, that will simply mean that they are gaining their independence. They're growing up!

Feel sad and miss them, but don't worry. They'll be back!

6

Getting
the Job Done

What is the single most difficult aspect of single parenting? The answer varies from person to person. I personally believe trying to fill roles that once belonged to your ex-mate is the greatest challenge of all.

A mother with full custody suddenly finds herself asked questions her husband used to answer. Which punishment is appropriate? What birthday gift would a teenage son most appreciate? How can little Jimmy improve his soccer game?

You want to relax on Saturday, but if you don't mow the lawn nobody will. The children watch you take out the garbage like Daddy used to do. You hear yourself yelling at your kids and feel out of control. You drive the car into the gas station, and ask for an oil change and a tune-up.

In the complete family, mother and father usually divide up responsibilities. Candidly, I don't think they are ever divided evenly. Moms always seem to have more than their share. But, traditionally, tasks are allocated something like this:

Father	Mother
Primary bread-winner	Part-time bread-winner
Home and garden maintenance	Housecleaning and washing
Vehicle mainte-nance	Shopping
Primary disci-plinarian	Children's transpor-tation
Weekend driver	Cares for sick children
Checkbook balancer	Checkbook balancer
Pet care	Pet care
Political analyst	Food preparation
Foreign policy	Clothes shopping and repair
Opens hard to open bottles	Deals with creditors
Watches sports on TV	Deals with school administrators
Makes foolish purchases	Buys necessities
Investigates late night noises	Hides from late night noises

I had to play with the list a bit to make it come out even! Films like *Mr. Mom* have had fun with the fact that men would rarely want to change places with their wives. Those men who have obtained primary custody of their children are the exception (only three percent), and their adjustment to single parenting is much more drastic than that of their female counterparts. There are countless things for which they are culturally unprepared.

The first step, before actually defining your role as a single parent, is to accept the fact that you simply cannot do everything well. If you try, you will spread yourself so thin that even the things you're best at will have mediocre results.

The second step is to accept a lower standard in areas where you used to excel. Look at it this way: You used to be a specialist of sorts and now you are a generalist. In short, do the best you can and don't worry about it. Nobody will fault you for not being perfect. And if you try for perfection you're going to drive everybody nuts—including yourself.

The third step is to look for substitutes who will handle tasks that your mate used to perform—gardeners, plumbers, electricians or friends who can fill in as "handyman."

The fourth thing you must do is find meaning in your new life, no matter how difficult.

From a cold, dark jail, the apostle Paul wrote some powerful words. They are secrets for happiness, and I really must share them with you.

> I am not saying this because I am in need, for I have learned to be content whatever the circumstances. I know what it is to be in need, and I know what it is to have plenty. I have learned the secret of being content in any and every situation, whether well fed or hungry, whether living in plenty or in want. I can do everything through him who gives me strength (Philippians 4:11-13 NIV).

Paul had learned to be happy even when his situation was less than ideal. That's what this Scripture is all about. But if you read it and then ask Christ to give you the strength to be Supermom or Superdad, you had better read it again! Christ created us with limitations so we would have to depend on Him. He gives us the strength to be happy within our limitations, but He never completely removes them.

We wouldn't need Him anymore if He did! At times, as a single parent, you will find out that things are beyond your capabilities. Fortunately, God only requires that we be faithful. We just have to do our best and trust Him for the rest. But for now, let's look at some practical things that will lighten the load.

1. *Opposite-Sex Questions.* When your child asks you something that would best be answered by the opposite sex, say "I don't know." Then write down the question. Send it along when visitation time comes and remind the child to ask the other parent

Naturally, you won't send questions that would humiliate the other parent like, "Why did Daddy leave us?" or "Do you think Mommy is ever going to leave that other man?" Include all sorts of inquiries, whether serious or lighthearted, that you think the other parent would really enjoy answering.

This will accomplish two things for your children. It will ensure that they are getting the perspective of the opposite sex. It will also help them respect the other parent. If you have no ex-mate available, then make a list of questions to ask another trusted member of the opposite sex.

Grandma and Grandpa, Uncle and Aunt, or close friends who have a little common sense will do fine. I think your pastor or a church youth leader would love to help you out in this way now and then. It will ensure "opposite sex input" and will benefit your child more than you can ever realize.

2. *Yard Work.* Gardening can be draining. If your husband used to keep a perfect yard and you have no teenagers to follow in his footsteps, you will have to innovate. There may be a single-parent dad who would

love to trade lawn mowing for a home-cooked meal and a little adult conversation. Just make sure that you are trading chores with someone who can be trusted. And make sure the individual with whom you're dealing clearly understands the terms of your arrangement.

If you can't find someone to help, then adjust. For one thing, irrigate as little as possible without killing your plants. This slows plant growth. Maybe you'll be able to work in the garden every other week, saving alternate Saturdays for other activities. Your yard won't be as lush as it was, but you will end up with three more hours a week to spend with your children. Learn to steal time wherever you can find it and give some of it to them. This spares them hearing those dreaded words, "Sorry, I'm too busy."

3. *Housework.* This should be a shared responsibility. Bear in mind that children are much more capable of helping than you probably realize.

- Four and five-year-olds can be taught to tidy up their rooms.
- Six and seven-year-olds can make their own beds, keep their bedrooms clean and help with washing and drying dishes.
- Nine-year-old children can take out trash, feed pets, do light vacuuming and dust. They can probably also help with the food preparation.
- Ten-year-olds can learn to do most of the things you can do—even their own laundry. Just keep them away from fire and blades until they are 12.
- Twelve-year-old boys and girls should be fairly self-sufficient.

When your children help you around the house, follow these simple rules. 1) Do chores at the same time every week so they know how to plan their schedules. 2) Let them grow into each responsibility slowly. You may have to show them what you expect of them a few times before they meet your standards. 3) Try not to let it become a demeaning time—assure them that what they have done is a bigger deal than what they haven't. 4) Provide an affordable reward. Anything from stickers to an afternoon at the movies will do.

Saturday may prove to be the best time for the house chores. The happiest, most well-adjusted children I have met during 25 years of youth work always did regular, weekly chores. If your children are in their teens and haven't yet been taught to do anything, you have got your hands full. Their values are formed and it is likely that you will have to move heaven and earth to motivate them to get to work. Still, for their sakes and yours, it is worth a try.

One more little tip—the house will probably not be as neat as it was when you were a complete family, unless you had a very sloppy mate. But remember, children won't thrive emotionally under the authority of a frustrated perfectionist. A little clutter never hurt anyone.

4. *Cooking.* Food preparation is your responsibility, but if your children are old enough, it can be shared. I had a 13-year-old boy in my office the other day. During our time together he mentioned that it was his night to fix dinner for the family. I asked him what he was making. "A roast," he said. Then he went on to name the vegetables, salad and dessert that would complement the meal. Upon further inquiry, I discovered that, at 13, he was fully competent to live on his own. What a great gift his mother had given him! He was so proud to be able to tell me he could do all those things.

When the dinner hour rolls around, make it clear that there will be only one mealtime and one menu choice per meal. That will save you a great deal of time and frustration, and will guarantee that your whole work force will be there to help you clean up. Plan your shopping carefully, too, and try to avoid more than two trips to the market per week.

5. *Transportation.* Children's activities may take you near the post office, library, cleaners or market. Try to think in terms of efficiency, and just make one trip if you can. That way more hours can be devoted to rest, relaxation and diversion.

6. *Car Repairs.* Vehicle maintenance may not be your cup of tea but it should not be avoided. Don't "just hope" that your car will hold together. It won't. Regular oil changes and lubrications can add thousands of miles to your automobile's life, and they are really very inexpensive. Tune-ups, when necessary, can improve gas mileage considerably. The money you will save in repairs is worth your small investment in timely maintenance.

These days oil should be changed about every 6000 miles and tune-ups should be done at about 10-15,000 miles. Just follow your car's manual or ask your mechanic to outline a plan for you.

7. *Family Safety.* If you are a single-parent mom and you hear night noises that sound potentially dangerous, call your local police department. The police are very helpful in such episodes, and there is no reason for heroics on your part. You have got no reason to prove that you can do anything your mate could do.

8. *Etc., Etc., Etc.* Don't become frustrated over life's daily little inconveniences. Henry David Thoreau was on to something when he exclaimed, "Simplify, Simplify!" There is a great gulf between what we *want* to do and what we *need* to do. Our requirements are not nearly as complex as television and print advertising

would have us believe. And the more we curb our wants and concentrate on our needs the happier and less frantic we will be.

The Single-Parent Schedule

"Bonnie Martin called," said my secretary Annie. "She asked if she could see you right away. She was crying, so I told her to come right in. I thought you'd want to talk to her."

"Sure, that's fine. Did you pick up on what might be the problem?"

"She just said she didn't think she could handle it anymore. I didn't pry because she sounded like she needed to get right in."

I reflected on what I knew about Bonnie's situation. She has three children, all under six. Her ex-husband is out-of-state. He's not paying any child support and Bonnie's parents live about 500 miles away. She never gets a rest from the kids. She's probably completely exhausted.

Fifteen minutes later Bonnie Martin came into my office and sat down. Her hands were trembling and her eyes were red from crying. Every time she tried to speak she failed because she was choking back tears.

"It's okay to cry, Bonnie, I have plenty of time. Let's just wait till you're ready."

"This is so stupid!" she said. "I hate it when I get emotional and can't talk!"

She wiped her eyes, breathed deeply and finally began. "Pastor Gary, I'm not even sure why I'm here. I just feel panicky all the time. I used to be a really good mother to my kids, but now I get shaky whenever they ask me for anything. I feel like I am going to start screaming and not be able to stop. I don't even know what's causing this. I used to handle everything really well, but now I can't. What's wrong with me? Am I going crazy or something?"

"Bonnie, you're not going crazy," I said softly.

"How can you be so sure?" She looked at me uncertainly.

"Let me ask you some questions. You just answer them honestly and quickly, yes or no. Okay?"

She nodded.

"Bonnie, do you ever hear voices?"

"No."

"Do you see things that other people don't see?"

"No."

"Do you think others are plotting to make your life more difficult?"

"No."

"Do you ever wonder whether anyone is following you?"

"No, of course not."

"Bonnie, you're one of the most normal people I've ever met! You answered no to all the questions. If you hadn't, I would be worried about you!"

"Then why do I feel like I am going crazy?"

"Let me ask you some more questions. What time do you get up in the morning?"

"Five A.M."

"What do you do at five A.M.?"

"Well, I get ready for work, eat breakfast and make the kids' lunches."

"Then what?"

"I wake up the kids and get them ready for school. I make their beds, fix them breakfast and do their dishes. Then I drop them off at the day-care center. Michelle and Michael stay there all day but Melinda is walked to school by the day-care center staff and picked up again at two-thirty.

"I go to work from 8:30 A.M. till 5:00 P.M. It's about a 20-minute drive from the day-care center. I pick the kids up at 5:30 P.M. if there are no traffic problems, or a little later if there are.

"I am a legal secretary and our firm is very busy, so everything has to be done 'right now.' Then, when I get to the day-care center, it seems as if all three children want all of me 'right now.' Yesterday I sat in the parking lot for 15 minutes just to get away from anybody asking me to do something. I felt guilty because I really didn't want to pickup the children. There have been times lately when I just wanted to go home and leave them at the day-care center for about a month! I really feel bad when I think that way, but I do sometimes."

I was getting tired just listening to Bonnie's schedule. "Bonnie, tell me what you do after work."

"Well, sometimes we stop at the store and shop for dinner, or maybe we just get milk and cereal. It takes a long time because all the kids pickup junk food, toys or books and beg to have them. They're tired, I'm tired and sometimes our store trips are not very pleasant experiences. I get witchy and say unkind things to them."

I couldn't help but smile. "Such as?"

"Such as, 'If you keep picking up stuff you're going to leave the store with no hands.' Or, 'Mommy's going to leave you in the trunk while she shops if you don't stop this.' One day I told them I was tired of having children and if they didn't back off I was going to take them to an orphanage. They would be like Annie before Daddy Warbucks came along. We had just rented *Annie* from the video store and they were pretty impressed. I told them Mrs. Hannigan was older and meaner now and would know exactly what to do with them!"

I laughed. "Good line," I said. "I wish I'd thought of it when my kids were younger. So what else do you do?"

"Well, I guess what everybody does. Next comes dinner, dishes, baths and putting them to bed. I try to get that done by 7:30, but I'm still yelling 'hurry up!' until after 8:00. Once they're down, I take a hot bath while the clothes are in the washing machine and dryer. It's my luxury time."

"What about the weekends?"

"Melinda has a piano lesson, Michelle plays soccer and Michael, my three-year-old, stays with me while I juggle the transportation. It seems like we're always running errands, doing shopping, birthday parties, house cleaning. You know?"

"Do you get any rest at all on Saturdays?"

"Sometimes I'd rather be at work. It seems that the kids need more of me than I have to give. Sundays are only a little better. When the kids go to Sunday school I go to church. I get away from them from 9:00 till Noon. I work in the nursery second hour because they need help, although I have to admit I'd rather go out for a cup of coffee with a real live adult and talk about something more meaningful than Gummie Bears and Saturday cartoons. Sometimes we take a nap on Sundays. I have them watch Sunday-night television programs while I do bills and finish cleaning up the house.

"When Kevin left us and moved to Arizona I was crushed but I was able to get everything done. Now I feel like I'm going to crack. What went wrong?"

"Bonnie, nothing went wrong! You've handled things marvelously well considering that you have had to be mother, father, provider, maid, nanny, chauffeur, playmate and nurse. You aren't going crazy, but you are exhausted and you are right on the edge. We have to find a way to get you some help. I have a prescription, although it may take a month to put it in place. Are you willing to try it?"

"Sure." said Bonnie, looking a little skeptical about the possibility that life could be different. "What do I have to do?"

"We'll start tomorrow. When you pick up your children, ask the day-care teachers if there are other single mothers like yourself, or even working mothers with two or three children. Talk with them and ask them if they would like to form a babysitting co-op. I'll talk with some of our single mothers here at church and see if we can organize some rest and play time for you.

"My suggestion is that you find at least two times a week to get away from your children for a few hours. You also need to think about dropping some things so that you are not always on the go. It's a great myth, thinking that kids need to be busy all the time. They don't. Actually most of the kids play soccer at school recess. Michelle wouldn't be missing much if she wasn't in a league. Melinda could wait to take piano lessons until she is a little older. One of my hardest jobs is convincing single-parent mothers that they aren't in a complete family anymore. Some things have to change. Next Sunday I want you to resign from working in the nursery. You need the rest far more than we need the help."

She nodded, and looked up at me hopefully. I wasn't finished!

"I want to hear that on Sunday you invited a girlfriend out for a cup of coffee during the Sunday-school hour. I want to hear that you talked about adult matters such as feelings, hopes and dreams, and that it felt good just being with a friend."

I continued to share with Bonnie some principles for a single-parent schedule. You can work your schedule out any way you want to, but here are some ideas. Be sure to include rest periods—and build in some friendship and play time, too.

For the most part, Bonnie just needed permission to do the obvious. Her schedule will never be a walk in the park, but it became bearable. If you are redesigning your own schedule, you'll want to consider these five vital needs.

1. Time for rest and relaxation, including some exercise.
2. Time away from your children. (This way you won't resent them when you are with them.)

3. Time for friendship. You were not made to be without human contact—*adult* human contact!
4. Time for growth. Reading, studying and special classes fall into this category.
5. Time for spiritual sustenance. You need the strength that prayer can give, and you must insist on making time for continuous nourishment from God's Word.

You may find it easy to resist this chapter. The answers could sound a little too simplistic. But I assure you that anything you can do to simplify your schedule may bring just enough relief to return you to your "coping level."

Of course, I'm not suggesting that you begin to neglect your children or any of your other responsibilities. But the more you rest and recreate, the better you will feel. And the better you feel, the better parent you will become!

7

Never Enough By the End of the Month

Most pastors have no use for an electronic calculator during their counseling sessions. For me, as a single's pastor, however, it is an indispensable tool. On a regular basis, out it comes as I try to help someone develop an achievable budget. Sometimes it's impossible to cover all the bases, but usually my singles and I are able to do something to make things work out. Maybe you too, could use some help in this very strategic area. As we mentioned before, economic devastation is one of single parenthood's most painful pitfalls. Let's consider three important principles before we lay out a budget plan.

You cannot spend what you do not have.

That may sound a little simplistic, but there's one big reason I mention it—*credit cards*. Credit cards usually lead to terrible problems for those who live below average standards of income.

If you are unable to meet the total monthly balance on your credit-card statement, you will be paying about 18 percent extra for whatever you purchase. You will soon be at your credit limit, and once you are there, you will have no way to pay off what you owe and nothing to use for emergencies. If you have a credit card, and are very responsible, keep it for severe crises only. If you tend not to be as responsible as you would like, put your card in the hands of someone who will hold it for you—for emergency use. Better yet, cut it up so you won't be able to use it. It bears repeating: You cannot spend what you do not have. And another thing...

As a single-parent family, you cannot maintain the same standard of living you once enjoyed as a complete family.

Single parents who can't accept this principle suffer the most. They end up squandering all kinds of time mired in self-pity, panic and envy. When we are forced to admit that we simply are unable to make it on what comes in, then the answer is obvious but painful—we have to cut back, cut corners, cut it out. Something has to go!

If you don't have a solid grasp of finances, then you may want to search through your four basic help groups for someone to advise you about financial decisions (see Chapter Five). Quick decisions are rarely wise or profitable. Let's look at some problems commonly faced by single parents and try to determine what choices are available.

Suppose you are a single-parent mother with two children. You have a boy, 12, and a girl, 9. Your total income, including child support, is $1600 a month. You are renting a three-bedroom house for $1000 a month. Your car payment is $180 and your food is costing you about $225. Your son requires orthodontia which amounts to about $100 a month. You also need $95 for medical needs, car repair, clothing for yourself and the children, utilities, insurance for your car and house, telephone and entertainment.

Guess what? You don't have enough money! And you probably feel hopeless. But there are some alternatives within this situation. You will have to make some decisions, because the situation demands it. And if you don't, someone else will. Your choices may not be ideal, but the sooner you can come to grips with what must be done, the sooner you will find a manageable lifestyle. Here are some possible alternatives.

1. You can move your daughter into your bedroom with you, then rent her room out, preferably to an older woman. The tenant would pay from $350 to $400 a month, which works out to spendable cash for you. Of course this solution carries with it a few new problems. You will have a loss of privacy, and you will have to deal with the possibility of conflicting lifestyles. If your tenant doesn't pay her rent, she creates additional financial problems. But taking in a renter is a possible solution.

2. You could move into a smaller two-bedroom house or apartment which would cost about $700 per month. That would give you $300 extra spendable cash. It wouldn't provide as much cash as the tenant, but you would be able to maintain your privacy.

3. You could search for a roommate with a similar situation to yours, and together rent a four-bedroom residence for $1100 a month. By sharing the expenses of rent, phone and utilities, your savings would be $450 a month, plus half of the utilities. That would give you about $550 additional spendable cash. You could also share babysitting, and would be able to cooperate in cutting financial corners in other ways.

4. Perhaps your son's orthodontia could wait a year or two.

5. If you need a chunk of cash, and have equity in your car, you might consider selling it and buying an older model. Just be careful! The repairs on a used car can eat up a lot of money, and the sale might not generate all that much cash anyway.

6. Some single parents have the option of moving in with their own parents. That, of course, might be your best alternative, if you can handle it emotionally. In that case, it could be a very good situation for both yourself and your children.

Now that we've looked at some examples, can you see my point? There are always ways to make life more manageable. I would caution you about one tempting possibility, however. Taking a second job is a dangerous proposition. You will use up a lot of money in child care, neglect your children and wear yourself to a frazzle. You will find yourself being a grouch all the time! I think happy and poor is a better state of affairs, all things considered.

There is a third and final principle to be considered.

You must set priorities in your budget.

This is crucial if you are going to make good decisions. Let's make a list of items that should be in your budget. I'll leave it up to you to arrange them in their order of importance.

- Housing
- Food (including eating out)
- Transportation (car, bus, gas, repair and maintenance)
- Medical expenses (doctor and dentist)
- Clothing
- Recreation (sports, boy scouts, girl scouts or related activities)

- Utilities (electricity, gas, phone, water and trash)
- Insurances
- Self-Improvement (lessons or classes of any type)
- Gifts to God and man
- Vacations or trips
- Savings for unforeseen expenses
- Anything you would like added, including present debts

After you have arranged them by priority turn them into a budget as follows.

Budget Worksheet

Write down your total income (that would include wages, child support and any other source of revenue).

Total income:

Now list, in order, your budget according to your own priorities.

ITEMS	AMOUNTS
1.	
2.	
3.	
4.	
5.	
6.	
7.	
8.	
9.	

ITEMS	AMOUNTS

10.

11.

12.

13.

14.

Total expenses _____

Subtract your total expenses from your total income.

Income
Expenses **–** _____
Final Total: _____

If your total budget was equal to or less than your total income you'll make it. If it was more than the total income you have to do some more work. Your first question, of course, is "Where can I cut?" Go ahead. Make those decisions! You might want to call a friend to assist you at this point. If your church has a business manager he should be willing to sit down with you and provide some suggestions. But remember, the ultimate decisions are in your hands.

Suppose that, even after cutting back, there is just no way you are going to make it. At that stage, you will have to decide what bills will have to wait. Maybe you will have to make partial payments. Perhaps you will have to do without something.

When you have too many bills and it's either pay them *or* feed your children, then let something go and feed your children. But remember, all of your debts represent promises, and you owe it to your creditors to work out some sort of long-range plan to pay them. Hard times do not excuse us from doing the right thing. Nevertheless, difficult circumstances may require us to postpone doing some things.

Whatever you do, be sure and communicate with your creditors! Do it even though you may be dreading any sort of hostility. Creditors have a right to expect us to keep our word. They will often work with us, not only out of compassion, but simply to minimize their losses.

There are two budget experts on the scene right now and you might find their books very helpful and practical. Larry Burkett has a national radio program that is excellent for everyone. Two of his books are: *How to Manage Your Money* (Moody Press, 1975) and *Answers to Your Family's Financial Questions* (Focus on the Family, 1987). Ron Blue also has an excellent text about principles of money management, *Master Your Money* (Thomas Nelson). You can't go wrong with either book.

Just a couple of more comments and we will move on. I strongly suggest that as soon as you receive your paycheck or support payment, you sit down and write out checks for your bills. That way you will avoid the temptation to fritter away your earnings. And another thing—pray. Pray that God will bless you with enough income. And don't be afraid to give.

No one knows your situation better than God. He has allowed it. If you can't give to Him, He is not going to sit up in heaven acting like Scrooge McDuck. He certainly doesn't need your money. Most of all, He wants you to trust Him.

Single-parent mothers are especially vulnerable to the threat that they are not going to make it financially. Theirs is a very real fear because they are so often faced with the reality of walking the edge of the Grand Canyon financially. If a car breaks down or a special medical need pops up it can trigger maximum personal insecurity. How often single women long for someone to take care of them! It is easy to start thinking, "If only I had a man, I wouldn't be in such desperate need."

Dana Sterling had two little boys, who were six and eight-years-old. She was a competent secretary but she only made eight dollars an hour. Even with minimal child support she could not meet her budget. Dana was not spending foolishly, but she didn't have enough money.

Dana was attractive, and a lot of men asked her out. One attractive older man who was quite successful in business was smitten with her and began driving her to the finest restaurants in his very expensive cars. It was refreshing for her to enjoy a more lavish lifestyle, and she found herself rather attracted to this silver-haired Prince Charming. He helped her meet several of her needs, and more and more she felt cared for and safe because of his presence in her life.

Although Dana had made a commitment to Christ, she was gradually placing her trust in Ray instead of in God. Ray seemed so close when any real need popped up. He was a persuasive man, and she was very vulnerable. She began spending the night at his beautiful home, and soon slipped into a constant violation of the morals in which she believed.

It was about this time she began coming to me for counseling. She was feeling deep guilt and wanted very much to please Christ with personal righteousness, but her fear of poverty overwhelmed her and she would not break away. Ray was beginning to "own" her, although he was not making a conscious effort to do so. He was simply playing out the values he understood. He would have said that he wasn't taking anything more than he was giving, and if Dana wanted to break it off she was free to do so.

Dana eventually gave up her small apartment and moved in with Ray, figuring that by doing so she could get her back-log of debt straightened out. Ray had invited her to live with him, but he had asked her not to bring her two sons with her, except to visit every other weekend. His own children were grown and, at 50-years-old, he didn't want to start his childrearing years all over again with Dana's small children.

Dana's husband was remarried and wanted the boys to live with him. Although he had abused her, he had never harmed them. She made the arrangements, but deep inside she hated what she was doing. The guilt over her immorality was compounded by the feeling that she was abandoning her sons. They were not exactly adored by their stepmother, and in fact, the eldest son was constantly at odds with her.

At this stage nobody but Ray was the least bit happy. And as time went by he, too, became dissatisfied. He reached a point where he didn't like to see the boys coming over at all. When they did, Dana noticed that Ray drank more. He refused to allow them to act like children. Everyone was walking on eggshells. More and more, Ray was playing the role of a father and he was not the least bit pleased. He complained to Dana about her inadequacies. She, in response, catered to him. The more she tried, the more he seemed to be pointing out her weaknesses.

Dana was now feeling morally corrupt, guilty for abandoning her boys and convinced that she couldn't do anything right. Although money concerns caused Dana to carry on her uncomfortable lifestyle, surprisingly she continued to come in for counsel. I could see that she was miserable, so miserable and desperate that she was beginning to consider suicide. I knew she wanted me to talk her into doing the right thing.

Fortunately she ended up choosing to trust Christ instead of Ray. She moved out of Ray's elegant home. She broke off the relationship and began to make do with what she had. She was able to survive financially. Before long, Dana regained the peace that comes with a clear conscience and she was healed from the effects of her immorality. A very fine Christian gentleman about her age took an interest in her and they began a wholesome and godly relationship.

Love blossomed, and after a sound engagement period and more than enough premarital-counseling time she was married—in fact I was given the honor of performing the ceremony. Her husband Grant is good and kind. He loves her boys for who they are and because they are part of her. The boys are now living with them.

Dana's story is typical. Too many women choose to work out their problems using their own schemes and solutions. When we depart from the counsel of God there will always be consequences, and I can assure you they won't be satisfying ones.

Please remember—be willing to be poor but happy. And let God care for you, not man. The payoff is up the road and around the corner. You can't see it now, but I can. So can Dana!

8

Wounded Lambs

You have probably noticed that along the way, I have repeated what must seem like a very harsh statement. I have said that children never really heal from divorce. I'm sorry to tell you that I really believe that to be true. But I also want to be quick to say that I believe children can rise above their wounds dramatically. It may help you to swallow this bitter pill if you realize that you are hearing it from a single-parent child, and a severely wounded one at that.

When I was seven- or eight-years-old, I remember my mother being very unhappy. I was never sure why she cried, but often felt responsible when she did. Occasionally she would have to be institutionalized for weeks at a time. During those weeks we would visit her in the Camarillo State Mental Hospital. She was clinically depressed, but I was too young to have understood her plight even if someone had tried to explain.

Needless to say, those trips to Camarillo are not among my fondest memories. When we visited, she would cry and beg my father not to leave her behind. They discussed ghastly sounding things like shock treatments, restraints, drugs and strange fellow-patients. When we finally did leave, we all felt guilty. She would hug us so hard it was embarrassing. You could tell she didn't want us to go.

My father had to take extra jobs to pay for her treatments. Consequently, my brother and I saw less and less of him. When we did see him he was exhausted.

My worst moment came in my 12th year. One afternoon I came home from school, threw down my book bag and headed for the refrigerator for a snack. I called out to my mother to let her know I was home, but there was no answer. That seemed strange because my mother never went anywhere. I checked out in the yard and couldn't find her. I went back into the house and began a room-by-room search, feeling there was something strange about the silence. I checked the living room and den, then headed toward my parents' bedroom.

As I passed the bathroom I smelled a strange odor and turned the light on to investigate. I was shattered by what I saw. Everything in the bathroom was covered with blood! There were bloodstains everywhere, splattered halfway up the walls.

I knew something terrible had happened, but I didn't know what. It was so horrible—there were pools of blood and it was *real* blood. I ran to the kitchen to use the phone but didn't know who to call.

I didn't want to scare my grandparents and I didn't want any of my friends to know. I sat down, put my head in my hands and tried to think of what would be the best thing to do.

I wasn't alone with my terror for long before my father came home. He looked very tired as he came through the back door. His eyes were reddened from weeping. Our eyes met but he looked away. He had been well-taught that men don't cry, and didn't want me to think he was weak. He put his hand on my shoulder and said, "We had to put your mother back in the hospital, Gary. This time she tried to take her life. You have probably already been in the bathroom. I was hoping I could get home in time to spare you from seeing it. She slit her wrists with a razor blade. She's going to be all right, but she'll be in the hospital a long time."

My father began to clean the bathroom. From time to time I looked in because I didn't want him to be alone. It looked spotless when he finished, but it never smelled the same again. The odor was a daily reminder of that horror-filled afternoon. How I hated that room!

After three months, Mother returned. But from that hideous day on, I never brought my friends home from school again. I was afraid of what they might encounter. I didn't want them to see my mother do anything crazy—I was afraid they would think I was crazy, too. I spent more and more time over at my friends' houses just to get away from the reminder that my home was painfully different.

Then my mother developed a new problem that was extremely hard to understand. Slowly but surely she lost the use of her legs. The doctors told her that it was "hysterical paralysis." They told her she could not walk because she didn't want to walk. I longed to believe her when she said it wasn't true, but she had done so many strange things that it was difficult. My father trusted her, though, and spent thousands of dollars on doctors who, after hearing her mental history, would simply echo the diagnosis that followed her around. By the time I was 15 she was using crutches and a wheelchair.

At the age of 49, the day before his 50th birthday, my father passed away. He had a heart attack in my mother's arms. He died right in front of my eyes while I stood begging the police to send an ambulance—fast! My father had worn himself out caring for my mother.

I loved my mother, but felt she was the reason that my father had died. I am glad, in retrospect, that I kept that thought to myself, and the day came when she was vindicated.

Several years later, after a history of going in and out of mental hospitals, a surgeon decided to do a thorough work-up on her. He discovered adhesions on her spinal cord. I'll never forget the look of relief on her face when she was told she could not and would not walk again.

For most people that would have been devastating news—but not so for Mother! She smiled. She hadn't been crazy about the paralysis, after all. She was acquitted! The adhesions would have been surgically correctable years before, when she was first losing the use of her legs, but now it was too late. They had a stranglehold on the spinal cord and always would.

Mother was vindicated, but was never able to cope with life's jarring disappointments. She had already lost my father, the last person on earth who wholeheartedly believed in her. Then, when she was 54, a man proposed marriage to her, and she accepted. He died of a heart attack two months before the wedding. That sent my mother into her final depression. She gathered together an enormous amount of prescription drugs and took them. No one found her until it was far too late. She died. She had tried to commit suicide seven times before, and finally succeeded when I was 27.

She left a note pinned to her chest. It was given to me when I picked up her personal effects. It read,

Unwanted, Unneeded, Unloved.

I want you to know that it still hurts deeply to tell that story. I am 45 today, and have never gotten over those hurts. From the time I was eight-years-old, nothing was easy for me. But God has given me the strength to overcome my past, including the fact that at different times in their lives, both my parents had serious drinking problems. My mother was also addicted to prescription drugs.

Your job is not to heal your children. Only God can do that. But you can provide them with tools to cope with life. First, you need to know what they are up against. They are wounded lambs, and they have been injured in many areas simultaneously.

The following is an excerpt from my book *The Divorce Decision* (Word Books). Its purpose is not to create guilt but to help you understand how divorce impacts children. If we can identify their sources of pain, we can provide help. I fully believe that the hurts and pain children suffer can actually be to their benefit, making them stronger and better. So read the following without guilt. Help is on the way.

The Children

If you have children of any age, they will be affected in an adverse manner by a divorce. To varying degrees, to be sure, but they will be affected.

Children have a dream to which they are entitled—at least in childhood. This dream we call "And they lived happily ever after." It has everything to do with how they view their future. If they gain the view that their future is uncertain and unpredictable, their lives will manifest several disastrous symptoms.

I'd Throw the Flowers Higher

Brandie and Stephen are children of divorce. On the outside, nothing is apparently different about them. They are both attractive, well-groomed and extremely active children. Stephen is nine, handsome like his father, and tan, as is typical for a California boy. Brandie is eight. She is blonde, sandy blonde, I would say, and has a generous number of freckles cascading down both sides of her cute pug nose. Brandie is refreshingly outspoken. When I met her for the first time in the waiting room at church she sized me up and said, "I can tell already I'm going to be bored."

I laughed and said, "Don't be so sure, Brandie. I used to work at a zoo and I have pictures all over my wall of the animals I used to take care of." Her blue eyes opened a bit wider, she shrugged and followed me down the hallway, as did her father and brother.

Dave had brought his children in because he knew something was bothering them, but they wouldn't tell him what it was. As most fathers, Dave was awarded custody for Friday, Saturday, and Sunday on every other weekend. The weekends were usually full of free communication, but for reasons unknown to Dave, his children seemed a bit depressed and subdued. Brandie would hardly talk to him at all.

When we sat down in my office, Brandie walked to my string bass that was standing in the corner. I could tell she was impressed with its size and more impressed when she plucked it. Her father was slightly uncomfortable with what she was doing, but I was very glad she was beginning to feel free in the office. After we began to talk, it became clear that the children were not going to talk freely in front of their dad. I asked Dave if he would step out to the reception area so I might talk to the children alone.

I knew that I might only get one opportunity to see them, so I tried to move as quickly to the problem as possible.

"It really hurts when your parents get a divorce, doesn't it?" I said quietly.

Stephen frowned and nodded his head in hearty agreement. Brandie's reply surprised me. "It's not so bad. Didn't bother me. You just get more moms and more dads. It's no big deal."

Stephen frowned and blurted out, "You're not telling the truth, Brandie. It hurt you a lot."

"Is that true, Brandie, did it hurt you a lot?" I asked.

"Yes," she said with her head bowed. "It would make me cry if I thought about it. So whenever I do, I take my thoughts to my secret place and lock them up. Then I don't have to think about it anymore. Then I don't have to cry."

"Have you put a lot of those thoughts in your secret place, Brandie?" I asked.

She looked up with sad eyes and nodded yes. Just for a second I wondered if she would begin to cry. She didn't though, and I wondered if she had just made a quick trip to her secret place.

I thought a minute and inquired, "Is your secret place getting full?"

She nodded and softly said, "Yes."

"What will you do when it gets full, Brandie?"

She didn't answer, and I felt moved to say to Brandie that crying was God's way of letting our problems out so they could go away.

I could tell Brandie was getting a little uncomfortable, and I let her change the subject.

"I don't say the F-word anymore," she said.

I swallowed, took a deep breath, and then probed, "What word is that?"

"F-A-M-I-L-Y," she replied.

"Family!" I exclaimed with both relief and surprise.

"'Gang' is the new word. People just come and go from a gang, and that's just the way it is. It's no big deal. It doesn't hurt."

"Do you dream a lot about your real mom and dad getting married again?" I asked.

Stephen and Brandie both nodded, and Stephen said, "Mom's going to get married to a new man. We don't like him very much. He's too bossy."

"What does he tell you to do?"

"He tells us what to eat for breakfast, just like he thinks he's our real dad."

"Is he over for breakfast a lot?" I asked.

"Just when he's too tired to go home at night."

"Is this what's been making you so sad—that your mom is going to get married again, but not to your real dad?"

They both nodded yes.

"But there is one good thing that's going to happen," said Brandie.

"What's that?" I asked.

"I'm going to be the flower girl for my mom's wedding."

"That sounds like fun," I said.

"You know what? If my mom would marry my real dad again, I would throw the flowers higher."

Brandie went on while Stephen nodded occasionally to affirm his younger sister's assessment of their future.

"You know what, Pastor Gary? My mom doesn't yell at the new man yet. But she will. And you know what?"

"What, Brandie?" I asked, wondering what she would surprise me with this time.

"She's going to start yelling at the new man, and he won't like it much and they'll get divorced. Then she'll get married to my real dad again." She smiled, sat back fully in her chair, cocked her head, folded her arms, and said, "Then everything will be all right again." She nodded her head again to show that was all she had to say.

You and I know that everything will not be all right again. In fact, there is a 70 percent chance that Brandie's mother will divorce again in five years. That means that they are likely to face the trauma once again. They will view the deterioration, feel the tension, and experience the fear of change, too much change, too early in their lives.

Deep, Worried Feelings

Butch is 12-years-old. We recently used him on a panel of children who were asked various questions about what it was like to go through a divorce. The specific question that Butch's answer stunned the audience with was, "What feelings did you have when you learned that your parents were going to get a divorce?"

Butch is a bundle of energy and a little sensitive to be answering in front of 300 adults. His father was in the audience also. He looked down, stammered a little, and finally blurted out, "I would lie in bed and listen to my parents argue, and then my heart would beat twice as fast as usual because I just knew one of them would come in and tell me that they were going to get a divorce."

Butch glanced quickly at his father and then looked down at the table. The audience was absolutely silent as they considered his answer. I could see in their eyes that they were wondering if their children had stayed awake with hearts pounding. Each parent considered to what extent their children felt anguished over the breakup of their families. I found myself teary, feeling for Butch and feeling for this group of parents. I wondered about the wisdom of having asked this question in front of a group of people who couldn't change the past and hoped that in some way it might impact the future.

I Don't Know If Anyone Loves Me Anymore

Recently a father shared a very personal moment he had experienced with his five-year-old daughter. The situation was that the marriage had been deteriorating significantly for more than five years. His daughter, Julie, had witnessed either harsh or no communication throughout her brief life.

Her parents were not staying together in the same bedroom. The intensity of the fighting had been accelerating, and Bob would simply leave the house rather than stay and be berated in front of the children. Sharon, his wife, would fall into depression and sit for hours doing needlepoint or reading the same page of the newspaper over and over again. The two youngest children were then left to more or less fend for themselves. Their diet had become one of cold cereal or quick snacks to tide them over until mealtimes (if there were mealtimes).

At 9:30 one night, Bob heard Julie quietly call out to him as he was walking to his own bedroom through their extensive hallway. He stuck his head into her room and gruffly asked, "What are you doing up?"

Julie reached up her arms and whispered softly, "Daddy, will you hold me?" Her voice was crackling and her eyes were moist in the corners. Bob pulled her close, and she said, her voice quivering with emotion, "Daddy, it's just that I don't know if anyone loves me anymore." Bob held her in his arms until she fell asleep, but before she did, he repeated over and over again, "Julie, I love you, and I always will."

I want to stop periodically and underline some specific points of consideration for you as you move through this section.

1. Divorce will leave your child with the inner feeling that his or her world is uncertain and unpredictable.
2. Divorce robs children of their fondest hope, namely, "And they lived happily ever after." Since they never really let go of this fantasy, it leads them through a series of disappointments.
3. The process of divorce, and it is a process not an event, produces a steady chain of excruciatingly painful events for children.
4. Because the parents are feeling such traumatic and dramatic pain, they are often without the ability to help others, even their own children. This of course leaves children wondering if anybody loves them

during the same period that their parents are suffering.

Tammy, in the next story, illustrates one of the tragic perceptions that children entertain. They perceive that somehow the divorce or separation was their fault. This is true about the vast majority of children, not only those I have talked to. Studies clearly show that this is a common perception.

Rich Buhler, the well-known radio host of "Talk from the Heart," shared a fact concerning all victims recently. He told us, "All of us, especially children, think superstitiously. We believe that good things happen to good people and bad things happen to bad people." This is true, and the more traumatic the event the more negative feelings children will have about themselves. Divorce is extremely traumatic, so divorced children are very subject to thinking they are worthless, hopeless and being punished. They think that this couldn't happen to good children. Rich called to mind the wonderful scene in *The Sound of Music* where Baron von Trapp proposed to Maria. She said yes, and then do you remember what Maria sang? "Somewhere in my wicked childhood I must have done something good." Now read Tammy's story with this in mind.

I'll Be Good, Mommy

Todd's wife had been gone five weeks. He had begged her not to go. He knew that they had lots of troubles, but probably not any more than anybody else. Todd had never felt this alone before. Had it not been for his four-year-old son and six-year-old daughter, he was sure that he would have taken his life. For them, he must be strong. They needed him more than they would ever need anybody again in their lives, and there was no way that he would let them down. His wife, Sherry, had let the kids down, too. They wondered what they had done that was so bad that Mommy didn't want to be with them anymore. For several nights Todd had rocked them to sleep as they quietly sobbed in his arms.

Sherry seemed desperate the night she left. She had managed to blurt out that getting married had been a big mistake. She had told him that she had never really loved him, but she married him just to get away from her parents. Her parting words were, "Todd, I've got to get away for a while. I have another chance to be happy and I'm just not going to miss it." She glanced at the children and Todd noticed a mixture of pain and guilt. She turned away and walked out the door. "I'll call you when I'm ready to talk," she said coldly.

She hadn't called. Tammy's teacher had called though, wanting to know what was going on at home to make Tammy so unhappy at school. Todd was embarrassed, but he explained to the teacher that Tammy's mother had left and he didn't have any idea where she was. He wondered what the teacher was really thinking. Maybe she was thinking he had been a terrible husband or something like that. She seemed nice enough though and promised to give Tammy some special attention.

Todd's most painful moment came the day after the teacher's phone call. He picked up Tammy from school, and she proudly showed him her drawing. It was clearly a house with four stick figures in front of it: a mommy, a daddy, a brother and a sister. Todd felt a twinge of pain. That was what he wanted their family to look like too.

"That's nice, Tammy. You are really a good artist."

Tammy looked at her drawing and nodded in agreement. She laid it in her lap gently and stared at it all the way home.

When she got home, she ran into her parent's bedroom. After several minutes, Todd wondered what she was doing in there. He stepped softly to his bedroom door and his heart broke just a little bit more because of what he saw. Tammy was holding her drawing up to a picture of her mother and telling it all about the drawing and her day.

"Mommy, this is what I drew today. This is what I want our family to look like. This family is happy. We could be happy again Mommy. I'll be good if you come home. I miss you Mommy."

Can you feel Tammy's hurt? Isn't it clear that she believes her mommy left because she had been bad? Tammy will spend years feeling that she is a bad girl because she feels that good things happen to good people and bad things happen to bad people.

I think you are getting the picture that divorce is a very devastating event in the lives of children. The following two poems were written by different girls, one 10 and one 15. The first we found in Mary Griffin's *A Cry for Help*. It was written by a 10-year-old being treated for depression. These poems speak for themselves. They are eloquent expressions of the emotional chaos children are forced to endure.

> Divorce shakes you off the ground.
> Divorce whirls you all around.
> Divorce makes you all confused.
> Divorce forces you to choose.
> Divorce makes you feel all sad.
> Divorce pushes you to be mad.
> Divorce makes you wonder who cares.
> Divorce leaves you thoroughly scared.
> Divorce makes a silent home.
> Divorce leaves you all alone.
> Divorce is supposed to be the answer.
> Divorce, in fact, is emotional cancer.[1]

The following poem was written by Jeni Goodloe when she was 15. She is lovely, the all-American girl, well grounded in her faith. Her poem was written in the midst of the reality of divorce.

Life

I had lost all my happiness,
All my joy;
My world was turned upside down.
I had to get out—
Get out and think things through.
I walked a mile or maybe two.
It wasn't long 'til I came upon some
    yellow daffodils.
Why so beautiful?
I asked myself.
Bright green grass,
Shining rays of sun;
All so comforting.
But then clouds started forming,
And rain began pouring,
The beauty was more beautiful than ever.
For now I knew what made the daffodils
The green grass so beautiful.
If there was no rain to make them grow
There'd be no daffodils to show.
So as with life; if there were no
Unhappiness to make us grow
There'd be no happiness to show.[2]

These two poems clearly demonstrate children working through the pain of a divorce. It is often as painful for children as for adults, and the effects are of a considerably longer and deeper duration.

A remarkable article ran recently in the *Orange County Register* entitled, "Ties That Bind: Divorce and Teen Suicide," by Bryce Christiansen. The article states that adolescent suicide rates have risen 300 percent during the last 30 years. This statistic had a remarkable correlation to the rise in the divorce rate during the same period. In fact, the American divorce rate has doubled since 1960, the article states. It would be impossible to separate the implications. The children of divorce are much more likely to take their own lives than children whose parents have stayed together.

Bryce states, "Once parents in an unhappy marriage stayed together for the children, but now more than two-thirds of those seeking divorce have children at home."[3]

Suicide is not the only problem that escalated because of divorce. Children who have experienced a divorce are absent from school at much higher rates than those who have not. They get lower grades and are much more likely to be discipline problems. Why? After most divorces, both parents must work. The children are mostly latchkey "orphans" from about 11 years on.

We have long quoted the saying, "The idle brain is the devil's playground." Latchkey children have far too much unsupervised time. As all humans, they will, if left uncontrolled, be likely to do what they can do instead of what they should do. It is fascinating to follow the performance of children in school as they are taken through a divorce. Their report cards act as an emotional barometer. I had heard that this was the case but needed to see it for myself before I was willing to put it in print. I asked a close friend if he could send me copies of his son's report cards. I wanted the report cards the year before his son became aware of the divorce, during the divorce, and the year after the divorce. They bore out the statements concerning the report cards being an emotional indicator.

Tommy was in the second grade during 1984-85. His parents were in counseling, but Tommy didn't know that: For all he knew, he was in the average American family. They went on vacations together, helped him with his homework, ate fast-foods and watched television. They attended church most Sundays and visited his grandparents with regularity. Tommy was oblivious to his parents' problems.

During 1985-86, Tommy was in third grade. His mother had filed for divorce, and his parents separated. An awesome custody battle ensued. Tommy was emotionally distraught. He wanted most to be with his father but didn't want his mother to think that he didn't love her. It was a hard year.

In 1986-87, Tommy entered the fourth grade. The court battles raged on, and he was examined by a psychologist to see with which parent he would live. He was shifted from home to home and was exposed to his parents' anger and depression. Life didn't mean as much to him anymore.

Compare the report cards and the comments. See if the effects of divorce are obvious.

Tommy's Report Cards

	Pre-divorce 1984-85	Separation 1985-86	Divorce Continues 1986-87
Reading:	B+	C+	C−
Mathematics:	B+	B−	C−
Spelling:	A	B	C+
Effort/ Citizenship:	A	B	C+

There were no teacher's comments in 1984-85. Comments in 1985-86 included the following: "Tommy is bright but doesn't work up to his capacity. He seems nervous and distracted. Tommy's work is inconsistent."

In 1986-87 there was a drastic drop in Tommy's study habits, and the teacher mentioned that she wished he would make better use of his time.

Tommy's report cards began to improve in 1988, but today he still shows evidence of a good deal of insecurity. In the fifth grade Tommy improved in most ways but showed an inordinate fear of being left alone and does not sleep well unless he can share a room with another person.

I interviewed a group of teachers from my son's elementary school and asked them if they could see visible or dramatic changes in behavior when a child was being taken through a divorce. The reaction was in itself dramatic and visible. Among the thoughts most often expressed were, "They look like zombies, staring out into space completely unable to concentrate." "They often become rebellious or perform negative behavior to gain badly needed attention." "They withdraw ashamed and embarrassed because they aren't living with both parents."

Statistics show a dramatic rise in drug usage in this group. One of the most dramatic moments of my ministry occurred in this context. I was called to St. Jude Hospital in Fullerton, CA, where one of the parents in our Single Parents Fellowship was watching her son fight for his life. He had contracted gangrene from a dirty needle while taking cocaine. Afraid to get help and expose his problem, he tried to treat himself and the gangrene got a roaring head start on the doctors. The infection had spread up his arm and down his back and the method of treatment was painful beyond imagination.

In addition to IV's and antibiotics, they performed daily surgery making long incisions so they might reach under the skin and scrape the infection off the muscles. They left the incisions open to drain and to be scraped daily. I can imagine no treatment more painful.

As the days passed, the doctors had expressed some concern that they would be able to stop the infection before it claimed this young man's life. Although they were divorced, both parents stayed at his bedside to support him. There was a great deal of tension in the room because the mother had been forced to take her former husband back to court for a large amount of back child support.

While their son was dealing with the possibility of his own death, the parents finally tangled over their financial problems. The phone rang. It was their son's best friend. He was calling to say that the drug dealer wanted his money, and he wanted it soon. If he didn't get it soon, he was going to do a little damage to the mother's home. Can you imagine the pressure on all the members of the family, especially the son, at that moment?

The son survived and seems to be making the adjustment to a responsible lifestyle after several confused years.

The unsupervised lifestyle of the divorced child leads to a predisposition to chemical dependencies. They lean more heavily on their peer group for their values, and if you haven't noticed lately, their peer groups are not a sufficient foundation for a value system. The current basis for the value system of the teen culture is drugs, sex and rock and roll. If children don't get their values from their parents, they will get them from their peers. And that is rarely good news.

Promiscuous behavior is likely if teens are left alone. They need to be loved, and if they are not, they will try to find love somewhere. They will be willing to experiment to achieve intimacy.

In many cases divorce can contribute to confusion in a child's sexual identity. It is now considered a fact that children establish their sexual identity between the ages of two to six years. They do that by watching their parents. When one parent is removed from the home, the one sexual presence is elevated and emulated. Values are developed during this period also, and parents are their children's primary source of values. So, for whatever reason, children are at a distinct disadvantage if they are raised by only one parent.

I Think You're Raising a Queer

Robby is now 41-years-of-age and scared to death. Robby is dying of AIDS. His disease is in its early stages, and most of the time he ignores it. Yet in the soft, quiet moments, his alone time, he is afraid to the very center of his being.

He contracted his disease from Merlin. Merlin was a pilot for a major airline. He died several months ago. He and Robby were homosexual lovers and had been so for a long time. Both were very promiscuous outside their own relationship. They played a type of Russian roulette and pulled the trigger one too many times.

The Robbys and the Merlins are often shaped by the major events of their lives. They are responsible for their choices to be sure, nevertheless, events may have predisposed them to bad choices. They will be held responsible for their choices, but so will the others who helped make them.

Robby's mother was Barbara. She married very young, at 18, in reaction to a brutal and abusive childhood. Barbara's mother divorced her husband three years later because she could no longer tolerate the beatings she received or his degrading alcoholism. Barbara only remembers seeing her real father five times in her life.

Barbara also married an abuser who was alcoholic. Within two-and-a-half years she was divorced. Even before they separated, he never stayed home and their son Robby was never exposed to a positive male role model during his childhood. Barbara was the only present factor in his young life.

Barbara's Aunt Rose was a crude, blunt, but honest individual. She looked Barbara in the eye one day and said, "Barbara, I think you're raising a queer. Robby never plays with little boys, he's always wearing your clothes, and he wants to be the princess in the school play."

Barbara didn't know what to think because people didn't deal with homosexuality 35 years ago. She had no idea what to say or what to do.

By nine-years-of-age, Robby was seeing a child psychologist for social maladjustment. He was a loner. The other children made fun of him and teased him mercilessly. During this period his younger sister, Beth, became very ill and received by far the most attention and affection from Barbara.

Barbara remarried when Robby was 13. The man she married turned out to be far worse than the first man she married. He had walked away from his first marriage when his own son was three. When his wife died, he was forced to take custody of his son. Billy was now 15 and had also been raised without the influence of a male for all those years. Billy joined Robby as a stepbrother, which turned out to be the turning point for Robby.

Billy was already acting out his homosexuality, and he introduced Robby to acting out his homosexuality.

From that time on, Robby considered himself a homosexual, although he consistently practiced bisexuality.

Billy, the stepbrother, was a bisexual and deserted three wives and several children during his pitiful lifetime. What a mess.

Robby had been practicing his homosexuality for years, but it was never confirmed to Barbara until her son was discharged from the Navy for homosexual panic. He thought the Navy had told his mother, but they hadn't. As she listened to his story, she was stunned. Aunt Rose was right, she had been raising a queer.

Barbara has for years lived under a strained relationship with Robby. Since his high school years, he has made it clear that he cannot stand her. He has taken delight in her humiliation and flaunts his homosexuality whenever he can. During a candid moment, he shared in despair, "Mother, I don't even know who I am."

Robby will most likely be dead by the time this material is published. It seems clear to me that his destiny was written in part by a process—divorce. Without a long explanation, let me suggest three other effects of divorce on children.

1. Children of divorce will be much more likely to spend time in jail.
2. They will experience more health problems, both mental and physical.
3. They will have much greater risk that their marriages will fail.

So there you have it. Once the divorce decision has been made, little lives are inevitably affected. Sad as it is, two-thirds of the people who make the decision to divorce have children. And those children are, no matter what anyone does to prevent it, wounded lambs.

9

Staying Tuned-In

I don't know about you, but for Carol and me, raising children was an endless process of teaching them the "right things" to do. My children were authorities on the "wrong things" by the time we got them! I wonder who taught them all about that?

Because children know so much about doing the wrong things, it is not in humanity's interest to leave them alone too much without something specific to do. This presents a problem for custodial single parents. They are forced to work for the sake of survival and can't always be there to supervise their children. It also presents a problem for single parents whose children are too old for babysitters, and yet, when left alone, have a well-developed capacity to find inappropriate things to do.

From the age of eight, I was emotionally abandoned. As I mentioned before, my mother was severely depressed, in and out of mental hospitals. My father was working weekend jobs to pay for psychiatric services. That left my older brother Steve and me with plenty of unsupervised time. Steve was born responsible and always seemed to conduct himself as a gentleman. He was four years older than me. My parents had more time to work with him. Whatever they did for him "took." Then life caught up with them, and they didn't have time to do the same for me.

The Devil's Playground

In my case, the idle brain was, indeed, "the Devil's playground." Playground nothing! My idle brain was the Devil's national park! In the seventh grade I was given the opportunity to join the school orchestra.

I really wasn't the orchestra type, but the alternative class had homework to which I was highly allergic. So I turned in my textbook and followed Mr. Palmer, the aging orchestra director, to the band room. There he invited his new recruits to try the various orchestral instruments. The violin seemed too feminine. The cello held no appeal, partly because the boy I would have to sit next to had a long-standing case of cooties.

Then a closet was opened revealing a string bass. It was love at first sight. When I first plucked the massive strings, I could feel the resonance rumble through my body. This was a *man's* instrument. It exuded authority and standing next to it made me want to call out, "I bet my instrument can beat up your instrument." I had made my decision. I would be a bassist!

In no time, Mr. Palmer had an eager crop of seventh graders pulling bows across strings and blowing enthusiastically into wood, chrome and brass. The sound was not unlike what would be produced if a group of children jumped up and down on a multitude of cats and parrots.

When I was young I used to think of Mr. Palmer as a dedicated teacher and lover of fine music. As I look back now, I wonder what dark sin he was attempting to atone for by locking himself in a room five hours a day with junior high musicians.

As much as I loved my new instrument, orchestra was not always fun and games, not by a long shot. With 21 new students, Mr. Palmer's time was very limited. We did more waiting than playing on most days, while he showed new students what to do. We were all told to stand or sit quietly while he worked with them. I can't recall what my problem was, but I had an all-consuming desire to fill silent moments with sound. Sometimes I talked, sometimes I plucked, and occasionally, I belched.

Mr. Palmer was a patient man but occasionally I noticed him casually glancing at the clock. I think he was waiting for the retirement bell to ring. As for discipline, he had a "line" and when a student crossed it, as I did on several occasions, he had a fiendishly effective punishment. The remembrance of it keeps me a better man today, and I have since wondered why our own prison system has not employed it for the rehabilitation of hardened criminals.

When I offended him sufficiently, Mr. Palmer sent me to his office. There is no greater state of boredom a human can experience than when left alone for 30 minutes or more in a band director's office. There were band magazines, all printed in black and white. You could go through years of them and not be sure you weren't looking at the same one over and over again. It was horrible for a person with my well-developed sense of cool. I knew in my heart that no picture of Elvis or Fats Domino would ever brighten this room, this desolate closet of musical mediocrity.

One day, again banished to boredom, I found myself searching Mr. Palmer's office for something different to do. I glanced under the desk but all I saw were his marching shoes. They were old and cracked by the moisture they had absorbed from years of marching the band over the football field. The toes were curled up and most of the brown dye was faded. Obviously, they had served Mr. Palmer well.

I looked up. My eyes suddenly fixed upon the wall-mounted pencil sharpener. It was full to the brim with shavings. "Something to do," I thought. I will be helpful for a change. I removed the pencil shavings chamber and reached under the desk to empty its contents into the wastebasket. As I did, I was again captured by the rustic marching shoes. I looked at the shoes, then at the shavings, then at the shoes. My boredom was about to end!

I poured half the contents into each shoe and reassembled the pencil sharpener. I carefully lifted each shoe into my lap and packed the shavings firmly into the toe area until I had clearly reduced their size by at least an inch. I replaced the shoes under his desk and giggled. I remember thinking, "This may have been the coolest event that's ever happened in this office."

About a week later I discovered just how well my joke had gone over. As I was walking out the door, Mr. Palmer grasped my shoulder and asked if he might talk to me for just a second. I knew in my heart what we would most likely be talking about.

"Gary, Gary, Gary," he began. "You're not in trouble, but I really must know if my suspicions are correct. Last Friday when I practiced with the band, I put on my marching shoes. They are like old friends to me, you see, and fit perfectly . . . at least they did until last Friday. That day the toes seemed awfully full, awfully full."

Mr. Palmer squeezed my shoulder harder, and just for a second I had the illusion he was going for my throat. Fortunately, he didn't. He continued, "When I removed my shoes my heart sank. You see, my wife had given me a special pair of socks made of white Angora wool for my birthday. I have a touch of arthritis and varicose veins, and those socks provided a feeling of warmth and support that make my marching days a little less painful.

Those white socks are now white socks with dark gray toes. The dark gray won't wash out, bleach out or come out with any cleaning solvent now known to man. Those socks cost my wife seven dollars." (This was 1956.) "Son, she has fire in her eyes."

"Now I'm not going to tell Mrs. Palmer who put the shavings in my shoes. But, Gary, were you the one?"

He really looked hurt as he stared deep into my eyes. I wasn't always good, but I wasn't a liar at heart either, so I hung my head and said sadly, "Yes, sir, Mr. Palmer. I was the one. I didn't know I would wreck your socks. May I buy you a new pair?"

"No Gary, I couldn't let you do that. I can still use the socks." He looked grim as he said, "Listen, Gary, if you want to live to be an eighth grader never let my wife know it was you!"

Mr. Palmer gave my shoulder a final squeeze, a sort of a "you're forgiven" squeeze. He walked into his office and sat down slowly, then leaned against his desk. It was probably one of those days when he asked himself why he had gone into teaching.

I felt terrible. Here was a man who, in every way, had been nice to me. In a thoughtless moment, an idle moment, I hurt him as well as his wife. The fact is, I know way down deep why I did it, even though 33 years have come and gone. I did it for the attention I would get from my peer group. Humor was the hook I used to fish for the attention I didn't get at home. I used it all the time—it was very effective.

If your children are left with idle time they will find plenty of ways to fill it up. Their ways may be more destructive than mine were. I have had several children in my office this year who have turned to shoplifting. One 15-year-old girl admitted to me, "Sooner or later I'll get caught and when I do, my father will pay attention to me."

You know, it worked? But now she has a police record. Drugs and the drug culture are a natural for children who feel starved for attention. Obviously reaching out sexually is very attractive for adolescents because it seems to provide the closeness that they so desperately need to feel.

Even though single-parent children are more predisposed to the idle-time problem, every family faces it—especially since so many women have joined the job market. During adolescence there are no guarantees that the best of kids won't blow it in a big way. Still, there are some things we can do to cut down the odds of that happening. If your children are already 13 or 14 and rebelling, these hints probably won't work. You may need specialized and professional help for that. But if they are 12 or under these suggestions will be very helpful.

1. Insist on meeting your children's friends. Whenever you can, meet their parents. Invite their friends over for dinner and get to know them a little bit. At this age you still have a right to have input or veto power in your children's lives. Use it or lose it!

2. Say "Yes" as much as you can to your children's requests, but don't be afraid to say "No" when you have to. When you say yes, stick with it. When you say no, stick with that, too. Try to stay away from "Let me think about it" or "Maybe," unless you want your children to work you over all day and all night! If you really don't know, tell them when you will decide. At that time answer them.

3. Find definite times to communicate with your children so that you know where they are at all times. Obviously, the older your children are, the more you will have to let them make their own choices. You should always be able to reach them, and they should always know how to reach you in an emergency.

4. While your children are still young, get them started at taking on responsibilities, and keep them at

it. When they get to be 16, it would be a good idea for them to find part-time jobs. Of course, you will need to know for whom they're working. Once they're employed, it will be harder for them to get into trouble. They also will be learning more and more about the real world and what it means to be responsible.

5. If you have neighbors or friends who live nearby, it may be possible for your child to report in to one of them, letting a trustworthy adult know that they're home safely or informing her as to where they're going. If these friends are close ones, maybe you could trade some extra favors for letting your child have a "check-in" point. If they are not that familiar with you, it may be worth your while to pay them a little something for being on "standby." Such an arrangement provides your child with the feeling that somebody knows and cares about his well-being.

Your children need to be accountable to you. And, in a sense, you need to be accountable to them, too. It is imperative that you keep the lines of communication open with them at all times. This can accomplish more toward keeping them out of trouble than you might imagine.

Talking to the Kids

The children of divorce are often put in a terrible position when it comes to communicating with their parents. The divorce is most likely the biggest single thing that has ever impacted them. Yet, if they talk about something related to the divorce with one parent, they feel as if they are betraying the other.

Another problem children face is that many parents are over-corrective, and very apt to tell them how they should or shouldn't feel. This is frustrating if a child is angry or hurt. He may want to talk to you about something that has wounded or enraged him, but he fears that you won't give him the right to his true feelings.

Don't cause your children to feel that their emotions are stupid or inappropriate, especially when it comes to issues relevant to your family's breakup.

Young people learn to hold feelings inside until they are ready to explode. They would like to talk to their friends, but are embarrassed that their parents "didn't make it." It's difficult for them, unless they have a real soulmate for a friend, someone they are sure will understand.

Whether they are dealing with the divorce or some other important issue, you should encourage your children to confide in you. But there are some specific rules you need to follow or they will never let you in.

1. Listen until your children have completely shared their feelings. If you don't understand, ask them to help you. Seek clarification. Statements like, "Did you mean...?" or "Could you say that another way? I want to understand..." are very helpful. They let your child know that you really care, and that you want to be sure you are grasping the problem.

2. Don't expect to solve your children's problems unless they are asking for help. It may be they just want to know that somebody cares how they feel. It helps children immensely just knowing you are interested. Try saying, "I'd feel that way, too, if I were you." Or "I can understand how you'd feel that way." In doing so, you will relieve the children of the kind of tension that keeps them from telling you the truth.

3. When you have something to say that you think would be helpful, ask for permission to say it. That way they will learn that telling you their personal feelings won't necessarily turn into a lecture. However, be assured that I am *not* telling you that you must endure abuse from your children. You get what you tolerate, and some parents tolerate way more than they should. Set rules for communication. You stick to them and make them stick to them: no foul language, no insults,

no lying, no yelling. On the positive side there should be love, openness, honesty and calm.

When you begin to communicate, it is good to take a bit of time with the children. Warm them up. Nobody does well when you walk right up and ask, "What is your deepest hurt?" Start with simple matters, then move on to the complex and personal. Don't be surprised if it takes you a while to see openness.

I have a close personal friend who works for the California public-school system. Her name is Naomi Landorf, and she counsels children who are showing signs of emotional damage. Over the years she has developed a formula that works well, moving children from the superficial into deep communication. She knows how to open them up. Let me share her system[1] and how it reveals important information. She asks the following questions:

1. Tell me what you would wish for if you had one magic wish? (Let them talk. Don't hurry them. It's a joy to hear what they might say.)

2. If you could choose just one person to go to Disneyland with who would it be?

3. What is the scariest thing that's ever happened to you?

4. What is the worst thing that could happen to you?

5. What is the best thing about... your teacher ... your class... best friend... Mom... Dad ... Sister and/or Brother... Self?

6. What one thing would you change about... your teacher... your class... best friend... Mom... Dad... Sister and/or Brother... Self.

7. What do you think your teacher thinks is best about you?

8. What do you think your mother/father thinks is best about you?

9. What do you think your best friend thinks is best about you?

10. What do you think your teacher would want to change about you?

11. What do you think your mother and father would want to change about you?

12. What do you think your best friend would want to change about you?

13. Describe the kind of family you will have when you grow-up.

14. Finally, she asks the child to rate himself/herself on a scale of one to ten. She has them make an x where they think they fit, first looking through their own eyes, then through their parent's eyes, and through their teacher's eyes.

Academic Scale

Ask your child where he/she would fit in a contest for grades in his class.

0-----------x-----10	self's rating
0---x-------------10	parents' rating
0------------x----10	teacher's rating

Appearance Scale

Ask your child to rate his/her appearance.

0---x-------------10	self
0-------------x---10	mom
0--------x--------10	dad

Now that you have taken the child through these questions, you can move with relative ease to the sort of issues you suspect may be bothering him/her. You might lead-in with queries like these: "It's really hard to go through a divorce isn't it?" "You know what's been hardest for me?" "What's been hardest for you?" "Are there any questions that you would like me to answer about the divorce?" "What do you most miss about the way things used to be?" "Is there anything that you would want to say to me if you knew I wouldn't get angry with you?"

You need to be warned that these questions may take you where you do not want to go! Children may require explanations you don't wish to give them. But in the long run it is better to bring all things into the light. This is what Scripture teaches us to do, and helping mend your children's emotional wounds is worth the risk.

In your talks, be as positive as possible without being insincere or indulgent. The one thing that you want to do is picture a better tomorrow. Insecurity is one of the enemy's best tools, so do what you can to disarm it. Watch Walt Disney's *Pollyanna* with your children. Pay special attention to the way "looking for reasons to be glad" changes a whole town for the better.

Being glad and keeping positive channels of conversation open in your home will have a great effect on your children. And on you, too, by the way!

10

Ready to Move On

When should you begin dating again? Some of the
most challenging decisions faced by single parents
involve the opposite sex. The biggest question is, "Am I
ready?" Fortunately, that is really not so difficult to
determine, since there are some basic guidelines, both
well-known and time-proven.

One oft-quoted statistic relates to marital bonding. It
is believed that, to unbond from a first mate, it takes one
year of healing for every four years of marriage. If you
are still attached emotionally, you are not ready to
rebond. As you move into a new relationship, it is almost
certain you will either be hurt or you will hurt someone
else. This is a general rule, of course. Just as we each
have individual recovery rates from serious illness, we
also unbond within slightly different time frames.

You will be greatly tempted to consider yourself
healed before you actually are. God's very first assessment of mankind's personality was, "It is not good that

the man should be alone . . ." (Genesis 2:18). It is natural to want to seek a mate.

But as you feel the tug of that natural inclination, try to temper it with the reality that marriage did not make you happy the first time. The odds are four to one that it won't the second time, either. You see . . .

- Second marriages have a 24 percent success rate within five years.
- Third marriages only succeed 13 percent of the time.
- Fourth marriages succeed just 7 percent of the time.[1]

This pretty well shoots down the myth that we learn by our mistakes. We are who we are and carry our weaknesses with us most of our lives. That caused Hegel, the German philosopher to exclaim, "The only thing that we have learned from history is that we have learned nothing from history."

The stakes are high. No one wants to be part of another failure—the cost is just too high and the pain too deep. One of the members of our single-parents fellowship said, "It's not remarriage that I'm afraid of, I just don't want to go through another divorce."

In a conversation with Charles Grodin, Johnny Carson was asked what the most personally devastating event of his life had been. Without hesitation he said, "My first divorce." Just about anyone who has experienced a divorce would say the same thing. That's why it is important for you to take this question seriously: Am I really ready to move on?

Time is an important indicator, but it is not the only one. Your attitude and feelings are a solid gauge of your readiness. Think your way through the following list. It will provide helpful guidance—practical ways to measure your own degree of healing.

1. *Am I now living more in the present than in the past?* Are you? Consider your thought life. Are you still spending time thinking, "What if I'd been a better mate?" or "What if my ex came back?" The number of "If onlys" and "What ifs" are solid clues to how you are progressing. Present-tense thinking deals more with "What will I do now?" and "How will it affect my future?"

2. *Have my periods of depression become fewer and farther apart?* No one completely escapes the depression that follows divorce. At first it hangs in gloomy clouds over every waking hour of your day. As time goes on, the periods of depression should lessen noticeably. Everyone has down periods, but only a few remain incapacitated for an extended time. If you are still overshadowed by depression, then you are not ready to move on.

3. *Have I overcome my tendency to look for nurturing or rescue?* If you are still seeking a caring Daddy or Mommy figure to "make it all better," you need more time. Far too many people use relationships as anesthetics. God should be our first line of defense. Then we ought to draw on our own coping mechanisms, the ones God has given us. Friends or lovers do not have it within their power to "fix" us.

And bear it well in mind—if we give them that power, we make it possible for them to break us again, too.

4. *Have I learned to live alone and not be lonely?* There is a big difference between being alone and being lonely. For most people, living alone would not be their first choice. Still, the feeling that alone is okay is a very healthy one.

5. *Am I spiritually secure?* We should have the inner feeling that God is caring for us, and that in His time things will come together. Such convictions are a significant indication of healing *if* they represent the way we

really feel. Caution is in order here, however. It is easy to *say* we believe we are spiritually on top of things, when it is actually the way we *wish* we felt.

6. *When problems hit, do I have a problem-solving attitude or do I overreact?* Explosive and uncontrolled emotions in the face of problems are a dead giveaway that we are still the "walking wounded." We are not ready to move on if we are still in this mode. If we are healthy, we will pray, seek responsible counsel and not overreact.

7. *Have I identified my weaknesses and am I willing to work on them?* Taking the time to work on our own personal inclinations before burdening someone else with them is a very important concern. This is really a matter of facing up to what part we have played in our past failures.

Ask yourself these kinds of questions:

- Did I yell too much or become icily silent during intense periods of communication?

- Were my spending habits responsible or did they create tension?

- Was I more concerned with my needs and feelings than my mate's?

- Did I have early childhood damage that kept me from being a healthy partner?

- Am I obsessive in my use of drugs or alcohol?

- Do I work too much?

- Do I have to be perfect and demand that standard from those around me?

- Do I have problems with lust that I periodically cannot keep under control?

- Do I need to be in control of those around me at all times?

- Do I have violent mood swings?

- Am I violent?

If you really want to be daring, try to remember the criticisms of your former mate and write them down. Ask yourself if there was any validity to his (or her) evaluation. If there was, admit it and form a game plan to deal with those issues for the sake of the future.

Let me add one thing—please don't become obsessive about attaining perfection. Do become obsessive about being open to growth and change for the better. God designed us to be more like Jesus, and made it a process more than an event. An open, humble attitude which realizes imperfection and seeks growth is very attractive.

8. *Am I thankful for the hard times?* We should be able to look back at our painful circumstances and acknowledge that they brought growth and refinement. We should be able to say, "God really has been with me! I can see the changes for the better now and I don't resent the scars." When the Lord tells us that all things work together for good, He isn't copping out. (See Romans 8:28.) It's true. Once you can see that, you're on your way. And believing before you see is just fine, too. That's called *faith.*

9. *Do I still entertain fantasies of reconciliation?* If you do, you should not consider moving on. It would be unfair to the next person. I have seen several cases where a person became fond of someone else while still bonded to a mate. When the mate wanted to reconcile, the still-bonded spouse returned, leaving the new love brokenhearted. It's not right to do that to someone.

10. *Am I ready to contribute to a new relationship?* The least healed are those most preoccupied with their own needs. True love frees you from the bondage of your own needs—without forsaking wisdom. The wisdom I am talking about is very essential, however: *Do not* look for another needy, wounded person to bond to! If you do, you will most certainly embrace a heartbreak.

11. *Do I consider myself complete with God, whether or not I ever remarry?* Is God my happiness and my sufficiency? A "Yes!" answer to this question means you are ready to graduate. If you truly believe it, you are healed. You can move on now—not because you need to, but because you want to. And you can do it with confidence.

When you move on there are guidelines to follow to make the best possible move for the future. You have to make the right choices. You will have to have a game plan and stick to it. The following list is neither complete nor perfect, but it has been time tested.

When You Look for a Mate...

1. Don't date people whose divorces are not final. They will not be healed, and you will see changes in them when they are. You may not like the changes! Besides, there can be no guarantee that they won't return to their mates if given a chance.

2. Make a list of those qualities that drove you crazy in your first marriage and make sure the person you choose is relatively free of them. We have a tendency to be attracted to the same kind of individuals over and over, but we don't have to be.

3. See what kind of relationship your new prospects have with their parents, especially the parent of the opposite sex. If you are not in a position to observe, listen to how Mom or Dad are talked about. Ask how mother

treats father and father treats mother. Chances are that's exactly how you're going to be treated.

4. Experience at least one full year of dating your prospective mate. It is hard to be on your best behavior with a person for a year, and you will want to see each other at your worst a few times. Why? Because it's not a person's best that is difficult to live with. You want to know the worst to consider whether or not your relationship can work.

5. If a person is in deep debt and you're not, wait until the bills are paid before getting married. There was a man in our single-parent fellowship who was charming, handsome, apparently kind, witty and deeply in debt. He swept one of our beauties off of her feet and pressured her to marry him right after she had been awarded a large sum of money in a lawsuit. They were married and he paid off his debts. The day—the very day—the money was gone, so was he! He initiated divorce six months after the wedding, leaving his new wife not only broken, but broke.

6. There are several differences to which you will want to pay close attention. Research indicates these differences can have a heavy impact upon the success rate of the marriage.

- An age difference of 10 years or more is not healthy. It may seem desirable to a person who wants to be mothered or fathered, but that desire will wear off all too soon. With that sort of an age spread, people are going through different stages of life at different times. They have unmatched energy levels. This can have a very negative influence on marriage.

   Love has never yet been proven to conquer all, and statistics indicate that age difference is a very real handicap. There are exceptions, of course, but be honest and ask yourself if it might be possible that you won't be one. The fact is, you probably won't. And in a second or third marriage, you will want to eliminate as many pressures as possible.

- Intellectual differences can pose problems for both parties. For the less developed or intelligent, it can cause feelings of inferiority, inspire jealousy and generate a need to control or dominate. For the more highly intelligent or developed, it can inspire feelings of superiority, eventually causing them to determine that their mates are boring, unchallenging and incapable of bringing out their best. I wish you could hear as often as I hear, "I put that bum through college and he dumped me." Intellectual disparity is a significant problem. If not now, it certainly will be later.

- Cultural and ethnic dissimilarities are significant. If there are language differences, you can expect communication problems. If your respective cultures frown on mixed marriages, your families will not provide enthusiastic support for your marriage. This is sad, because there are no moral or biblical grounds forbidding intercultural marriages. Such disapproval results from everyday prejudices. Nevertheless, intercultural marriages fail at a very high rate.

- Don't believe the "Brady Bunch" myth. The more children each party brings to a relationship, the less chance the marriage has to survive.

  Poor communication is the number one problem in first marriages, stepchildren are the number one problem in second marriages. Don't ever be tempted to underestimate children's ability to drive a wedge between you and your mate. You begin your marriage more bonded to your children than you are to your mate. That's why kids don't like stepparents.

And be sure of this. Everything changes when you move from engaged to married.

- Living together before marriage to "see how it works out" strikes a potential death blow to the eventual marriage. We now know that the couple who cohabits before marriage has an 80 percent higher divorce rate than the couple that doesn't. The couple that waits for intercourse until marriage has a far higher success rate than the not-so-chaste couple. Generally speaking, we should use things and love people. Test driving a car is reasonable. Test driving a person is ludicrous.

- Religious differences are very critical. People who have a deep faith will want to share it with their mates. It is heartbreaking when they can't.

   Christians are forbidden to marry nonChristians. The Bible says, "Do not be unequally yoked together with unbelievers" (NKJV). I wish I could tell you how many times I've been told about disappointing marriages where men and women really could not share their faith. I have been asked to warn people of the future sadness this kind of relationship brings, when the magic of moonlight runs its course.

- Having general things in common is valuable, or you will find conflict in how you spend your time. At first sexual attraction and shared painful pasts will draw you together. But if you wait till all that wears off, you will discover whether you are truly compatible.

This is really a very basic list, but I think it is important none the less. If any of these built-in troubles are present in your current relationship, it doesn't mean you can't make it "till death do us part." It just means you will have to work much harder at keeping things together. And remember, you will have to work very hard anyway if your second marriage is to succeed.

Dating and the Children

Children of various ages will react differently when you begin to date again. And children's reactions to their parents' new companions are generally negative for a myriad of reasons. Think as a child would for a minute and you can understand why.

First, young children sense that the time and affection once theirs is about to be given to someone else. Older children are more territorial, but still fear the loss of affection. Both young and old boys and girls often see dating as the final death blow to the previous marriage, a forewarning that their real parents will not be getting together ever again. It is the nail in the coffin to the fantasy "And they lived happily ever after." Children have an intuitive fear of the unknown and the idea of a stepparent is often more than a little scary to them.

There are children who feel a need for another parent because the missing one fails to give them any attention. They will be all for your remarriage and, in fact, can become vulnerable little matchmakers.

Because of all these considerations, I suggest that, until you are very serious, you keep your dating life separate from life with your children. When you begin to date, you can give them "news reports," and keep them posted as to the progress of the relationship. But I strongly recommend that you keep them separated from the person.

Once you are convinced that the person you are dating is a strong candidate for marriage, then arrange a meeting. As time passes, share positive little stories about your friend so your children will begin to form a positive mental image. Don't create a "superperson," causing eventual disappointment, but do be positive. What you are doing is providing time for them to adjust to the idea of the relationship existing at all. They need to become resigned to the idea that you are moving on, and, therefore, so are they.

Some questions may arise in the minds of the children when they know that you are moving on. Anticipate some of them. Once you feel the time is right, invite them to ask all the questions they would like to. Below is a run-through of a hypothetical "announcement" made at a family meeting. Let's visit a single parent named Doris. She is the mother of a high schooler, Janet; a junior higher, Ben; and an elementary school child, Sandy.

"Children," Doris begins, "As you know, I have been dating a man named Curt Stevens. At first it was just a friendship and we had a lot of fun going places and talking together. Well, as time has gone on our feelings have grown from friendship to love—romantic love.

"We haven't made plans to marry or anything like that but our feelings are serious and might develop that way. I thought it was time for you to know.

"First of all, I want you to know that this new friendship certainly won't mean that I'll love you any less. I have a mother's love for you and a sweetheart's love for Curt. He is also my friend. I'd like it if Curt could be your friend too. He's very nice, you know. We may stay friends or we may someday be married—it's too early to tell. But you will be the first to know if we do decide to think about marriage.

"But if that should happen, I want you to know that Curt will never be your father. Your relationship with your father won't change at all because of Curt. It would be nice to have a man in the house, though, to open jars and fix things. He could also help you with your homework sometimes in subjects I haven't been able to help with.

"Curt is a vice-principal at Canyon Oaks High School in Ferndale and he has two high-school-age daughters who live with his former wife. He doesn't get to see them as much as he'd like to, but he loves them very much. In fact he loves children a lot and he is a lot of fun to be around. He is a pilot and has a small airplane that he flies during the weekend. I'd like you to meet him next Saturday. How about that?"

Janet looks a little hurt. "Mother why didn't you tell us sooner that things were getting serious?"

"Well, Janet, I wanted to, but I felt it was better to wait. I decided that I would only bring a man to meet you if I thought I could be really serious about him. It's been hard enough on you kids. You have enough on your minds without worrying about my dating. Besides, up till now I haven't dated anybody worth mentioning."

Ben appears to be a little irritated, and Doris can see something is bothering him. Doris asks, "Ben, what's wrong? Remember? We agreed at family meetings that we would say what is on our minds."

"Mom, does this mean that there isn't any chance that you and Dad will get married again?"

"Ben, I know that you would give anything to see your father and me back together, and there was a time when I felt the same way. But my love died. After your father stayed with Julie for more than a year I knew that I had to start over. Even if he wanted to come home, and he doesn't, I'd be afraid he would leave me again. Ben, it's hard to ask you to give up a dream, but please—try not to picture your father and me together. It's just not going to happen. I'm sorry, Ben."

Doris hugs Ben and kisses him on the cheek.

Ben shrugs, tells her he knows it wasn't her fault and that he'll try to understand.

Sandy, the elementary-school-age daughter asks, "Is Curt handsome?"

Doris smiles, and cocks her head and says, "Well he's not as cute as Paul Newman or Tom Cruise but he's got Freddie Krueger beat by a mile."

Sandy isn't finished. She adds, "Will Curt ever try to spank us?"

"No, Sandy, he never will. He will be involved in discipline but spanking will be my job."

The children all agree that it is time for them to meet Curt. They decide to get together at the airport the following weekend, and to take turns riding in his plane.

Setting Boundaries for Dating

Guidelines for dating are important even when no children are concerned. They are mandatory when children are involved. Maybe it would be helpful for us to make one more list. These are wise boundaries, and many are scriptural ones.

1. *Display romantic affection only when you are away from the children.* For children who are still wanting to believe that your former mate will return, such affection is threatening. Teenage boys who have, in their minds, filled the male role in the home are super-threatened by affection. They become jealous. There is no need to provoke that. Once you remarry, introduce affection slowly, over an extended period of time.

2. *Try to balance the time that you date alone and the time you include the children.* The children will become resentful if they feel you are abandoning them for a sweetheart. You both need to find out whether your relationship will stand up in the presence of the children anyway. Don't forget—they are the leading cause of divorce in second marriages.

3. *Remain devoted to purity in your relationship.* You have no right to high expectations for your children's

behavior if your own life doesn't measure up. Sexual intercourse is meant only for marriage. It is worth repeating that those who work on saving intimacy for marriage have a better chance of a "till death do us part" arrangement.

4. *If you are thinking of marriage, set a reasonable wedding date.* Mark your calendar for a day not less than one year from now, and no more than 18 months away. Only very exceptional people with exceptional circumstances should wed sooner or later than that.

5. *Ask every question in the book about the person you are getting to know.* A relationship headed toward marriage should be open and honest to the max. Tell the other person all of your expectations for marriage—such things are better discussed before the wedding than after!

Many single parents believe that they've been vulnerable and transparent because they shared their deepest feelings about their marital break-ups. That has little or nothing to do with the success of the next marriage.

Ask questions! "What are your greatest fears?" "What dreams do you yet want to fulfill?" "Who is going to do the checkbook?" "What would you expect from me sexually?" "What's your dream marriage?" Ask whatever comes to your mind and encourage your sweetheart to do the same. The more you know about the person you are with, the more profitable your time together will be.

Let me close with a sobering thought. Children of single-parent mothers have been the subject of much study lately, and some fascinating results have emerged. Researchers studied three groups of children:

A. Children of single mothers who avoided or were given no opportunity for romantic involvement.

B. Children with mothers who moved in with men.

C. Children whose mothers remarried.

The following is a quote from *Psychology Today*, March 1989.

> Isaacs and Leon evaluated the children for behavioral problems and for social competence—how well they managed in their friendships, at school and in play. Surprisingly, the researchers found that it wasn't children in stepfamilies who were the best adjusted, but children whose mothers steered clear of romance. Children whose mothers lived with a partner fared the worst. Their teenagers in particular had a difficult time socially.
>
> The researchers suggest some possible reasons that having a parent living with someone else creates problems for children. Without the commitment that marriage signals, children feel insecure about a relationship with a new man. Additionally, a father who objects to his children residing in a live-in arrangement may communicate his disapproval. And the children, especially teens, may feel awkward about morals.[2]

I always feel good when modern psychologists discover an age-old truth. It's so healthy for them! These studies reveal how God intended us to be, and how violating His laws can have serious consequences that affect our children's lives.

My personal feeling is that pursuing romantic interests, when it is timely and appropriate, can be fine—*if* you proceed with wisdom. Your objectivity and your feelings must be part of a family team effort. This will help you make a wise choice for your future. Of course

God's Word says clearly, "If any of you lacks wisdom, let him ask God..." (James 1:5).

Intense and fervent prayer is needed when making a decision of this nature and magnitude. Seek the counsel and guidance of both man and God. Dare to ask Him to make you miserable if you are making a bad decision in a remarriage choice. Don't be afraid to learn the truth.

How much better for God to make you miserable than your new mate!

11

The Winner's Heart

What is the most meaningful decision you make each and every day? The following quote will give you an idea how Pastor Chuck Swindoll answers that question.

> This may shock you, but I believe the single most significant decision I can make on a day-to-day basis is my choice of attitude. It is more important than my past, my education, my bankroll, my successes, my failures, fame or pain, what other people think of me or say about me, my circumstances or my position. Attitude is that "single string" that keeps me going or hinders my progress. It alone fuels my fire or assaults my hope. When my attitudes are right, there's no barrier too high, no valley too deep, no dream too extreme, no challenge too great for me.[1]

If you are reading this book, it is because you want to succeed as a single parent. I want to echo the truth—a right attitude is the closest thing you will ever have to a formula for success. There are a number of very practical helps and assignments that will assist you, but none of them will take you as far as a right attitude. Before you begin to act upon the *things* you can do, please consider the *thinking* you can do.

In our single-parent program we have had some exceptionally meaningful moments. Ours is an honest group and so our times are often deeply personal and very touching. One evening we invited a young mother from another church to share how God was helping her cope with the awesome task of single parenting. Her name was Mary Campo. She had none of the credentials of our usual guests and was not on any speaking circuit. The truth was, when I first met her I saw nothing that set her apart from our regular Tuesday night crowd. Nothing, that is, until I took a closer look.

The closer look revealed two things. I noticed eyes that sparkled with life, and a relaxed posture that reflected an inner feeling of deep and abiding peace. Mary's time of sharing came and I fully believe that her 15 minutes before our very large group were among the most remarkable moments we've ever had. Here is what she said.

When I was first asked to share what God is doing in my life as a single parent, I felt the same way that you might feel if you were in the middle of remodeling your home—if you had walls torn down, doors off hinges, paint scraped off and the place was a plaster disaster. I feel like a friend has just invited a group of people over to see how God is doing with me. Well, I'm finding out that God loves to renovate. He has been doing a lot of renovating in my life these days. And it hurts!

It hurts to have walls torn down and paint scraped off and doors off hinges, so that people can look in and see the mess. But I believe that God would have me invite you to come and see my mess. Because if I don't, you will only see the outside of the house, and there is no power there. That is not where God is working. The power is in my weaknesses. His power is perfected in weakness. Right now, as a single parent, I feel very weak. Essentially, I have been a single parent for five-and-a-half years now. And I want you to know that I am tired.

I hate trying to juggle all the responsibilities of single parenthood. I hate the responsibility of the upkeep of the house, yard and car. I can hardly describe to you how weary I am of the financial strain, barely squeaking by every month. And that's only because I keep putting off doctor and dentist appointments and car tune-ups and a growing list of various needs. Oh, God sends the faithful manna every month. But, like the ungrateful and rebellious Israelites, I want more. I have been doing day-care in my home for four years now. And some days I feel like if I change one more dirty diaper, or wipe one more runny nose, I will just fall apart.

And doesn't it get lonely? How I long for a relationship that will fill this emptiness, and make me feel complete as a woman. There are two people in my life who qualify me for single parenthood: my daughter Christy, and my son T.J.

Christy is a beautiful girl of 10, creative and witty, and she has a tenderness and sensitivity about her that goes beyond her years. This was born of earlier times, of living in the confusion and loneliness of being five-years-old and watching Daddy leave. Mommy was too wrapped up in her own pain and coping systems to comfort that frightened child. Today, no matter how many times I tell her I love her, I feel as if I've barely scratched the surface of her need. When I tuck her into bed at night, we hug, and she never wants to let go of my neck.

"Please stay and talk with me tonight, Mommy!" Her need of me is so great that it makes me want to run away.

"Not tonight, Honey. Mommy's tired."

How often these words haunt me long after she's fallen asleep. How many nights I've cried for the lost opportunity of assuring and comforting her with my presence. Weeks turn into months, turn into years, of lost opportunities. I have been too frightened to enter into her pain. It's so easy with children to make believe that "it's not there."

My son T.J. is a strapping, handsome boy of six, with a vivid imagination and dancing eyes. But years of uncertainty and unsettling changes have left their mark of fear. I know that his playful nature longs to break through the bonds of insecurity that force him to keep his emotions in check. The wounds seem so deep and I don't know where to begin, so basically I don't begin. It's so easy to say to a six-year-old, "T.J., maybe tomorrow we can spend some time together, learn to ride that two-wheeler (it's long been dormant in the garage), or go to the library, or play spies or baseball together."

But tomorrow is always in the future. Somehow it never becomes today. And I see how I try to fill up my time with things and people that don't carry painful memories for me. By excusing my children's needs away, I can avoid facing their pain and my own. Except that it never really goes away. And there comes a point when it's too much to push down any more.

There is a universal truth among us . . . that is that we all have pain! We all have heartbreaking, soul-shaking, spirit-aching pain. We may hide it, deny it, run from it, stuff it, wallow in it, mask it as anger, express it through depression, try to deaden it with relationships outside of God's will or timing, but it's there. And none of those ways of dealing with it will set us free from it, because God say's it's the truth that sets us free. And when we use those defenses to cover up the pain, we miss God's answer. Truth! The truth is Christ—Christ is the Truth!

He is the One who brings good news to the afflicted. He is the One God sent to bind up the brokenhearted, to proclaim liberty to the captives and set the prisoners free. He comforts all who mourn. He gives a garland instead of ashes and a mantle of praise for a spirit of heaviness. The answer for single parents is Christ alone.

I am discovering that any other way: relationships, friendships, cigarettes, alcohol, drugs, work, church involvement, chocolate-covered peanuts, any other source will not heal my pain. It will deaden it for the moment. But God is determined that we are to feel it. For He desires us to know the power of His healing. The overwhelming awesomeness of His reviving touch. The power of His resurrection life. God receives glory through the works that He has performed in us.

The people who have let God resurrect them from their pain are the people who carry the fragrance of the risen Christ everywhere they go. The unmistakable peace and presence of the living God surrounds them. They find the transformation that God is working in them to be far more desirable—a million times more desirable—than the devices they once used to mask their pain.

And so Mary concluded her eloquent message.

As a single parent, the task ahead of you is hard. Like Mary, you will be tired, frustrated with the financial strain, haunted by the feeling that you are going to fall apart, and at times you will feel loneliness stab like a frozen knife. You cannot face this task alone. And you will need to remind yourself constantly that you are *not* alone. Christ is with you if you belong to Him. He will strengthen you.

I have two primary mentors, both of whom have impacted my life for Christ more than anyone else. Both have been there to cheerlead through the hard times.

Lorraine Austin is a woman of great wisdom and the most interesting Bible teacher I have ever heard.[2] One evening, she told us about her way of dealing with situations that were far beyond her. She said, "When I get the feeling that I'm losing it, ready to fall apart or explode, I close my eyes and repeat over and over till I believe it, 'I can do this and more also because of Christ who strengthens me.' I say it out loud so that I can hear the sound of my own voice."

This is what is called self-talk. But let me tell you, it is not a technique invented by modern psychology. It is a far more ancient wisdom than that. It is called faith! It is acting positively upon God's promises to care for us. It is trusting in His power to get us through.

My father-in-law, George Burch, is my other mentor. He is always pointing out to me the sufficiency of Christ. He has convinced me that Jesus owns me, and what He owns He will take care of completely, so that I will be lacking in no good or needed thing.

Belief, *true* belief, always provides the foundation for proper action. So reminding yourself that Christ will provide the answer—and in fact *is* the answer—is profound wisdom. And by the way, He is the only real source of true healing in the universe.

Job knew what it meant to suffer and wrote some of the following thoughts. Read them and be reminded that God is your only hope.

> Do I have any power to help myself, now that success has been driven from me? (Job 6:13 NIV).

> In his hand is the life of every creature and the breath of all mankind (Job 12:10 NIV).

But he knows the way that I take; when he has tested me, I will come forth as gold (Job 23:10 NIV).

These three verses from Job express three truths I want you to believe with all your heart.

1. You and I don't have the strength to succeed in life if we live apart from God.
2. Our lives are fully in God's hands.
3. God hasn't lost track of us. In fact we are a part of a plan to become better people.

Our single-parent fellowship has adopted a theme verse. Please memorize it! You will need to remember it. Times will come when circumstances won't make any sense at all to you. You will wonder where God is in all the chaos. As you recall this verse, you will become aware that He is in the middle of everything, restoring order "in His time." Be sure to insert your own name into the verse—it is a personal promise for you.

"For I know the plans I have for you [   ]," declares the Lord, "plans to prosper you and not to harm you, plans to give you hope and a future" (Jeremiah 29:11 NIV).

In case you've been wondering lately, God is on your side, as well as on the side of your children. And that is a well established fact! But remember, just as a winner's heart is important to the one who competes, clear and visible goals are equally necessary. Are you running toward a goal, or just running in the proverbial rat race?

Goals and Objectives

When I worked at the Los Angeles Zoo I knew exactly why the zoo was there, and I could tell anybody who asked. Our first objective was to preserve rare and endangered animals for future generations. Second, the zoo existed to educate the public concerning wildlife and its need for protection. Finally, the zoo provided low-cost, wholesome family recreation. In each of these areas, our zoo was fulfilling its reasons for existence and was achieving the goals its founders had set up for it.

One day I felt a little troubled when I realized that I could clearly define the zoo's purpose but could not, with the same clarity, define the goals and purposes of my own family. The goals we had at the zoo gave us a solid, well-defined framework on which to build. But what was guiding the building of my own family?

I think that it is of great value to set some simple, achievable goals for your family so that you can keep focused on what is important. There shouldn't be too many points, and they should all be reachable. When I finally sat down with my wife Carol, we chose these goals for the upbringing of our children.

1. We wanted to raise children who loved God and had received Christ as their Lord and Savior.

2. We wanted our children to be responsible and hardworking.

3. We wanted our children to be able to form deep and long-lasting friendships.

4. We wanted our children to be obedient to us and to other people in authority over them (except where that authority was in conflict with their consciences or the laws of God).

5. We wanted our children to laugh at the right things and to be happy with a clear conscience.

6. We wanted children who were caring and sensitive to the needs of other people.

7. We wanted children whose convictions were stronger than the pressures their peers would exert on them.

8. We wanted children who could develop their potentials to the fullest and could make positive contributions to the world in which they live.

Knowing where you're going doesn't insure that you are going to get there. It does give you something to aim for, however, and it will impact what you do and how you do it. In our case we have raised two youngsters, and are still working with one. Our children, at the writing of this book, are 24, 21 and 14. We are very proud of all of them. They are not perfect—in that way they take after their father—but they do have good batting averages when it comes to the above list of goals. For that, and much more, we are thankful to God.

Take a little time right now and jot down goals and objectives that you would like to see your children working toward. It's nice to have the feeling that you are helping them arrive at a worthwhile destination.

Goals for My Children

1.
2.
3.
4.
5.
6.
7.
8.
9.
10.

There is no magic number of goals and I only left room for 10. I don't think most of us could remember more than that. It is wise to keep the number of goals condensed, so that you are able to keep them all in mind.

Eventually your children will choose their own objectives. At that point, it is important that they have a good foundation upon which to build. They will pick up their values from what you do, not from what you say. Take another look at your list and ask yourself a very hard question: Have you set goals for your sons and daughters that you have no intention of fulfilling in your own life?

If the answer is "Yes," you must do one of two things. Either scratch the goal off the list or consider changing your own lifestyle. My father did that for my brother and me—he changed his life for us.

My father was a heavy drinker before he got married. He stopped when he had children. He didn't want us to struggle with alcohol in the same way he had. He knew we would follow his example so he was willing to change his life to provide the high standards we needed to emulate.

I value truth because my father told the truth. I value hard work because my father valued hard work. I love people because my father loved people. By the same token, I eat all the wrong foods because he ate all the wrong foods! (Don't trouble your children with rules you don't keep yourself!)

The most concise statement concerning man and his purpose is found at the end of the Book of Ecclesiastes. For 11 chapters, Solomon labors to determine what life is all about. In chapter 12 he gives us his conclusions:

> Remember your Creator in the days of your youth, before the days of trouble come and the years approach when you will say, "I find no pleasure in them" (Ecclesiastes 12:1 NIV).

Solomon's point is, You'd better focus on the things of God when you're young, or life will give you no joy when you're old. Now is the time to pour yourself into your children. Like us, they won't be very moldable when they are older. If you already have teenagers, you know all too well that what I'm saying is true.

Finally, as you refine your goals, bear in mind that all of them must have their roots in the Scriptures. Think of the closing statement of this powerful book of wisdom.

> Now all has been heard; here is the conclusion of the matter: Fear God and keep his commandments, for this is the whole duty of man. For God will bring every deed into judgment, including every hidden thing, whether it is good or evil (Ecclesiastes 12:13,14 NIV).

Proverbs, Ecclesiastes and the Book of Matthew, chapters five through seven, are excellent biblical books to read. Study them, and underline important portions while you are contemplating what important principles should be incorporated into your children's lives.

Your goals will not be different from those of complete families, but your method of achieving them may be. And your attitude—your winner's heart—will be strategically involved in the process.

While you are "running the race," let the Church help—in fact ask the Church for help. If they won't assist you, find one that will. Be sure to ask every question you can think of, and learn from those around you.

As a matter of fact, if you will read on, you may come across some of the very questions you have been wanting to ask.

12

Some Difficult Questions

You will want to take a long, thoughtful look at the following questions and answers. All of them were submitted by single parents. Each one represents a typical and troublesome dilemma. And, unfortunately, there are no satisfying solutions to some of them. In many cases, the only approach any of us can take is to minimize pain and friction. I'm quite sure that you will find some of your own puzzles and predicaments woven in among them.

Explaining Parental Disinterest

"What do you tell your children when the other parent shows no interest in them?"

The answer depends on the age of the children and whether or not a child was inquiring. If the child was young and wanted to know "Why?" I would look for the least painful truth.

Let me share some reasons that fathers (and occasionally mothers) don't make contact with their children. The parent may simply be selfish and irresponsible. In that case, I would tell my child, "You are the best child a parent could ask for. It's not your fault! When Daddy (or Mommy) left, he was very mad at me, and he still doesn't want to talk to me. Maybe he will want to later, and then he'll see you, too."

Or, "Daddy isn't thinking too clearly right now. He's lost his way for a while, but later, when he finds it again, he'll want to see you more."

In some cases parents are mentally ill. They may have broken under the pressure of the divorce. If that's the case, I tell children, "Mommy (or Daddy) is sick in a special way that makes her unable to think right. Let's hope she gets better soon. When she does, she'll want to see you more!"

If the children didn't ask, but I sensed that a parent's absence was troubling them, I would ask them to tell me how they're feeling about it. If they said "I feel bad," I would say, "That's the way I would feel too. I'm sorry you're hurting." Then I would hug them. After allowing them to say all they want, I might share some of the previous statements. Then I would ask them why they think the other parent isn't coming around more.

It is tricky, but you will want to avoid criticizing the other parent while still conveying that the children are lovable, and that the problem is not their fault. You will need to sharpen your diplomatic skills!

If the children are 12 or older, I would ask them about their feelings and then simply listen. I would give them permission to feel, then I would suggest they write their feelings in a letter and send them to the neglectful parent. It may solicit a positive response. Or, sad as it is, you may verify that there isn't much feeling there for the child.

If there is very little affection evident, then you'll have to deal with the consequential pain. Most of us spend a lifetime trying to verify, one way or the other, that our parents love us. You may have to say things like "Your father just doesn't have it in him. It's not you—it's everybody. He just doesn't know how to love."

Stay away from ugly language. But if the children use it (except for profanity), permit it for awhile. Then encourage them to forgive the neglectful parent. Just don't force the forgiveness issue on them immediately. They will have to get over their anger first, and that may take awhile, as you well know. Be patient.

Explaining Immoral Relationships

"What do you tell the children about a parent who is immoral and violating Christian values?"

A young mother said it very well to her six-year-old boy, "Jeff, your Daddy wants to be with another mommy more than he wants to be with me. So he is leaving home. I hope he comes back, but I can't tell you for sure that he will. He loves you very much and I love you very much. You can see or talk to either one of us just about anytime you want to. Do you have any questions, Honey?"

When boys and girls are young, I don't recommend spending too much time pointing out the sins of their parents. Later, when they form their own values and beliefs, they will come to understand who was the "bad guy" and who was the "good guy." I hope they choose your values, but that will have a lot to do with how attractive you make them.

If you are bitter, legalistic and vindictive, you're going to make a real case for the adulterous parent. If you paint a scarlet "A" over the other parent's home, you will make the child feel supportive of evil every time he goes there. If too much is said, children feel miserable during visits, as if they are betraying the innocent mate.

When children are older, and have formed their moral codes, they will probably be angry with the immoral parent for a while, and then finally forgive. They need to live with both parents and show them respect, whether or not the parents are respectable. You should offer them a chance to share their feelings and offer to answer their questions.

Avoid discussing sordid details which would be hard for them to understand or forget. If they ask you, go ahead and explain that what the other parent is doing is wrong. Just don't say too much. And please, don't tell your small children to ask the adulterous parent to answer such questions. Older children, whose morals are formed, should have that right, however.

Taking a Necessary Break

*"I know I need to
get away from my children.
How much time is too much time away?"*

That depends on several variables. First of all, with whom would they be staying while you're away from them? If that someone is a loving, nurturing grand-parent, no problem. Take whatever time you need in order to return to your children refreshed and ready to serve them. This probably won't amount to more than two weeks.

Another important question: How damaged are your children? If they are terribly insecure, then that would shorten the time you would want to spend away from them. Young children are usually very clingy after one parent leaves the home. Just think what might go through their minds if they see you leaving, too! When you leave, call them frequently and write a postcard every day. You may even want to write to them before you leave and have someone give them your letters daily.

Once, when I spoke at a camp, I left cassette tapes of myself reading from my son's favorite books. I was gone for a week. Carol switched on the tape recorder and turned the pages while my son listened to my voice. She told me it was a lifesaver. Leaving small surprises for them to open each day is a good reminder that you love them. And, of course, they'll be expecting a little some-thing upon your return!

If you feel as if you're emotionally on the edge, or like life just isn't worth living, get away if you can. Remem-ber just two things: Your time away should be governed by the quality of care the children receive while you're gone; and be sure to keep in touch!

Handling Manipulative Behavior

———————

*"It is easy to
let my children manipulate me
because they're hurting. What do I do?"*

———————

Francis Schaeffer once said, "We get what we tolerate." If you let children manipulate you, they will become more pitiful than the divorce itself made them. Given the choice, I would rather have wounded children than selfish children. Permitting selfishness is no cure for divorce pain. Love and discipline are necessary remedies, and if you choose not to give them both you will see your children's powers of manipulation increase with passing years. Such skills will haunt you as reminders of your failure to parent properly. All children manipulate. It is a manifestation of a selfish, fallen nature.

If your inclination to indulge your children's desires is inspired by guilt, then ask their forgiveness as well as God's. The only thing guilt should inspire is repentance and humility.

If your disposition to give in to your children comes from pity, then give them the kinds of gifts that will build strong characters. Your assignment hasn't changed, only your circumstances. Single-parent children demand more discipline, not less; more sacrifice, not less. God understands the pain of watching a Son suffer, but He did not indulge His Son's request to remove the pain of the crucifixion. And aren't we thankful that He didn't?

Addressing Feelings of Shame

"How do I help my children
feel less ashamed about Mommy and
Daddy's breakup?"

This question is not an easy one for two reasons. Feelings are natural and do not change easily. A divorce is a sad thing and children do not like being a part of a sad thing.

When my father died, I was 15, and it was hard for me to admit that I didn't have a father. Although I had had a father, and a good one, that awareness was somehow not good enough for my present pain. It took a year or two for me to realize that everything was going to be okay, and that no one looked down on me because my father had died. In fact, I learned that kind and caring people actually gave me more attention when they discovered my father had died.

I had a harder time when my mother was institutionalized. I didn't understand the nature of her illness and wondered if people would think it "ran in the family." Fortunately, time healed me, and, once again, people's compassionate responses helped immeasurably.

Here's an idea that has worked in some of our families. While your children are sitting at the dinner table, take out a dozen eggs. (Preferably hardboiled ones!) Get a marking pen and have your kids draw happy faces on eight of them and sad faces on four of them. Now arrange the eggs in two groups of six. Mix up happy and sad faces in both groups.

Say to them: "See these two groups? The one on the right contains families just like ours where a divorce has happened. On the left are families like ours was before, when Mommy and Daddy lived together. Do you see how many are in each group? They are just the same. That's how it is with the children at your school. Half of them will be just like you. I bet you can't look around and tell which ones are like us now and which ones are like we used to be.

"The reason for that is this: There are happy and sad children in both groups. Most children would rather be in the left group and that's okay. But it's normal to be in either group. Nobody is weird because he is on the right side or the left. And, since none of them selected which group they were put in, it's not their fault where they ended up. I don't always like being in this group either. But we're still a family and we can still be happy."

This can be a difficult subject because we want to be careful not to make divorce seem too natural or too right. You might want to add to your speech, "When you grow up, you can try your hardest to stay in the best pile. That will please your children and make me happy. Best of all, God will be happy too."

Saying "No" to Visits

---

*"What do I say
when my child wants to be with the
other parent and can't?"*

This question has many possible answers depending on the situation. If there are dark reasons why your child can't be with the other parent, you need to be very careful what you say. If the other parent was abusive, a drug abuser, a sexual offender or mentally ill, then your best bet is to make it the responsibility of the court.

"Bobby, I know how much you want to see your daddy, but the judge and the court made a law that we have to obey. They said that, for now, you can't see Daddy until he gets well. We don't know how long that will be, but it could be a while. We have to obey the law. So, I'm sorry, but for now you can't see Daddy. But Bobby, I promise I'll tell you if they change the rule."

If your mate is out of state, communicate that neither of you can afford the expense of travel.

If your mate is in jail or in the service, help the children understand that Daddy is somewhere where he can't be visited by anybody.

If your children are impulsive, and you don't want to be driving back and forth to indulge their immediate needs, then, again, appeal to what the courts have decreed. Children sometimes need to overcome desires for immediate gratification—especially when it comes at your expense!

However, you always need to listen for heartfelt needs. If you ask them why they want to see Dad or Mom, and they reveal something of a deeper nature than usual, allow them the visit. It doesn't hurt to make some exceptions.

Introducing the Opposite Sex

*"How do I introduce my children
to the opposite sex when there's no one
in our lives to fit that description?"*

1. If there is a teacher of the opposite sex who teaches your child's grade, ask if your child could be in his class. You might want to talk with the teacher a little before doing that, however. Make sure he would be a positive role model.

2. If your children have grandparents living nearby, allow them to spend as much time in their company as possible. I believe they usually provide the best influence on the children, although there are exceptions. Uncles and aunts can be terrific, too.

3. Boy Scouts and Girl Scouts are positive and viable options.

4. See what your church has to offer in adult-supervised activities. Church youth directors were my greatest influences when I was a single-parent child. God also provided a special family that took me into their home when my mother was institutionalized. The Duncans helped me to see how life ought to be lived in a family. I saw God's love unforgettably demonstrated in that home.

5. Join a single-parent group that plans activities for children. At our church we have "S.P.Y." which stands for Single Parent Youth. They have weekly activities, and there are always men present who are participating in their weekend visits.

6. Sports leagues abound for boys and girls, and they are filled with adults of both sexes. Specialty organizations are everywhere. In our area, a child could be involved in anything from agricultural projects to computer clubs. Each organization is filled with adults who love children and enjoy spending time with them.

Making Custody Decisions

"How do you know who would make the best custodial parent?"

The mother is usually the best custodial parent for young children—not always, but usually. The kind of men who are awarded custody are a special breed. Only three percent of fathers get their children half the time or more When boys and girls reach adolescence, they may feel a compelling need to know the other parent. Wise and unselfish parents allow that to happen, regardless of the court decision.

If you are unwilling to give up custody, but don't have a good reason for stopping your child from living with the other parent, you may see rebellion and hatred develop. That doesn't need to happen. Talk with your children at length, until you understand why they want to make the move. Listen like you have never listened before. Think and feel what your child thinks and feels. At least be willing to cooperate with a trial visitation period if there is no blatant reason why it shouldn't happen.

There is another reason for you to exhibit willingness to give up custody. Perhaps you don't have a great deal of ability to control your children. They may need help from the strong hand of your former mate. If you can't give it to them, at least be willing to give them up to someone who can.

Using Children as Weapons

"How can you avoid using your children as weapons against your former mate?"

You must set up strong boundaries for yourself. You will damage your children for life if you use them as weapons. Follow these simple rules and you will be okay.

- Request that your children not tell you anything that your ex-mate would not want you to know. If they do, scold them for it.
- Don't poison your children against their other parent in any way.
- Don't withhold visitation for late or nonexistent child support. Let the courts handle that matter for you.

- No spy assignments should be given to your children—ever!
- Children should never be used as pawns to bargain for financial purposes.
- Don't betray confidences that would hurt your ex-mate intentionally. For example, don't tell your ex-husband: "Johnny says you acted like a jerk this weekend!" There is no place for that kind of nonsense.
- A subtle sabotage that affects the way your children view and treat your ex-mate comes from passing statements such as: "If your mother loved you she wouldn't have left us." Or, "If your father loved you he would pay child support." Or, "Your father is spending more time with her kids than with you guys."

Naturally, a list like that could go on forever. It would make you sick if you could see the way children are used to attack the other mate. It's appalling, and it's not how Christ would have us act. He told us to do good to those who use us badly.

Keeping the School Informed

"How much should you tell your children's school about your home situation?"

It is important that you be very honest with the pertinent school representatives. No doubt your children's behavior will change. Teachers and school personnel need to know why. If the reason for a behavior change is explained to them, they will work more willingly to resolve it.

Teachers see the devastation of divorce all the time. They know your child's world has been turned upside down. Furthermore, they know what to do to help. By all means, let the school people know what has happened, and that you need any help that can be provided.

The teacher is the best one to talk to, but it would also be wise to inform the counselor or the principal. This is a common problem for schools, and they are equipped to handle it. They even have professional counselors who will talk to your children and help them understand what they are going through.

Confronting Unfair Teachers

*"What do I do if my child
is negatively labeled a 'divorced child'
by a judgmental teacher?"*

If you feel that your child is being unfairly treated as a result of stereotyping, begin by confronting the teacher in love. If you get no satisfaction, go to the principal. Be ready to admit that your child may be making his own situation worse. Turn your attention to helping the school survive your child rather than supporting your child's terrible behavior.

There was a haunting phrase in a poem I read during the 60s. "Dr. Jekyll in the school yard, Mr. Hyde behind the barn." I was like that. I was fine at home, but my parents would have had no reason to defend me at school. I was a pill and there was no doubt about it. Try not to be defensive, and listen carefully to what the school has to say about your child before you form a battle plan.

As a last resort, after a thorough investigation, you might consider a class or school transfer. Let's just hope that your son or daughter won't be going out of the frying pan into the fire.

Discussing the "Other Man" or "Other Woman"

---

*"What do I tell the children
about the person with whom my mate
is having an affair?"*

Your mate's lover has probably been told that your marriage is over, that you are a monster and that your spouse never should have married you. She (or he) is most likely operating under that assumption, and your mate is the one responsible for providing the information.

In cases where children have been embittered against the ex-spouse's friend, they will feel horrible every time they are in the presence of the other person. If they act rudely, they may be treated rudely. You don't want that to happen. Say as little as possible about the other person. If your child asks you a specific question, answer honestly, but be brief and kind.

Making Holidays Work

---

*"How do we
work out the holiday schedule?"*

Hitting two places on the same day can be both physically and emotionally exhausting. Your child could learn to hate Thanksgiving and Christmas! I would set up the holiday schedule on an odd-year/even-year basis—this year with Dad, next year with Mom. Do make sure both sets of grandparents have a chance to see the children when they want to. This is usually just as important to the children as it is to the grandparents.

Birthdays could be the exception. Allow the children to choose what they want to do on birthdays, without either parent laying a guilt trip on them.

Letting Feelings Show

*"Should I permit my children
to see my emotions?"*

The answer depends on the intensity of your emotions. If it is sadness we are talking about—tears and soft crying—the answer is yes, by all means. If we are talking about loud, uncontrolled weeping and wailing, I think not.

Seeing how you feel gives your children permission to feel. Seeing you out of control, especially in our Western culture which values decorum, scares them witless. If we are talking vengeful anger, loud yelling and bad language, the children should never be involved. (It's not so good for you either, by the way!) The Bible has a general rule that applies here: "All things in moderation." Try your best to remember what it was like to be a child.

When I was a boy, I expected my parents to cope. My father fulfilled my expectations. For years, however, my mother frightened me by crying for hours and by attempting suicide on several occasions.

The answer from my point of view, is to let the children see some honest emotion. But hide the rest for private times with adult friends or counselors. Best of all, share your tears with God. His Word says, so beautifully, that He keeps all our tears in a bottle. And it is His deep desire to bind up the brokenhearted.

Working Out Visitation Logistics

"With regard to visitation, what is the best arrangement for picking up and dropping off children?"

The best way is for former mates to control themselves and be civil when present at the other person's home. When that is not possible because of high levels of anger, then find a well-supervised drop-off and pick-up point where you will not need to see each other.

Picking the kids up at school after class is fine for those whose employment makes it possible. A day-care center or a friend's or relative's home is also suitable. Churches provide good neutral territory. You could make a rule that the pick-up or drop-off person simply stays in the car.

We might expect these guidelines to furnish sufficient protection from incidents. Unfortunately, they may not. Several women in my group have asked the police to be present during exchanges. That usually happens during raging court battles, when money and children are still up for grabs. If it's any consolation to you, this problem usually works out after a year or two.

Considering Broken Promises

---

*"How much should you say
when your ex-mate doesn't follow up
on promises made to the children?"*

I would give the children permission to be angry about it. If it becomes a pattern, I would tell the children that their father or mother means well but is very forgetful. Teach them to be grateful whenever the parent keeps his (or her) word, but not to count on it happening.

You should try to stay out of the communication loop. Most likely your ex-mate doesn't do well with your criticism anyway. Encourage older children to say something to the forgetful parent if you believe that it might do some good or make them feel better.

And by the way, if you are the one that doesn't keep promises, hear this: In actuality, you are lying to your children. And you are teaching your children to lie, too, because they get their values from you. You are also telling them they are not important and you really don't care about them. Please don't make commitments you don't intend to keep. Get your act together!

Allowing Children Choices

---

*"How much input should children
have in visitation matters?"*

I think from the moment children begin to express their opinions, their thoughts ought to be heard and valued. The older the children, the more weight their opinions should carry. If both parents are known to be responsible people, then a 12-year-old should be able to choose with which parent he wishes to live.

Children ought to have a suitable reason to generate the change. "You don't let me do enough stuff," is not a good enough reason. "I miss Dad and want to be with him for a while," is more like it.

These kinds of moves should be for a prescribed time and, if there is a new mate involved, can only be worked out if that person is reasonable. Money isn't really the issue here. Child-support considerations should be a lower priority than the happiness and welfare of the child. In other words, sacrifice, if necessary, for the good of your children.

Custodial care changes are among the most painful decisions you will ever make. They should be made slowly, and should not be associated with recent emotional outbursts that may pass like a bad weather front. Prayer and more prayer, for strength and wisdom, should precede your decision.

In the first section of often-asked questions, we answered those that had to do with the children. Now we want to turn to inquiries that deal with the single parent.

Approaching the Breaking Point

————

*"How do you hang in there
when you just can't handle it anymore?"*

————

When you begin to feel this way, you are literally walking the edge. You are near your coping limits. Although, in most cases, you can maintain a good deal longer than you think, you are in the yellow "caution" zone and need to do one of two things. You either need to get help or you need to drop something you're doing.

I'm sure I've had a hundred—maybe two hundred—single-parent mothers ask me, "Do you think I'm having a nervous breakdown?" Not one ever broke down, and for a very good reason. They all took Pastor Gary's "prescription." They either backed off from some of their activities, or they got help. On a handful of occasions, women needed long-term professional counseling which, in every case, was effective. Not one chose suicide and not one cracked.

Are you willing to make some changes? Let me list the things that help most when you are walking the edge.

1. Adequate rest.
2. Physical exercise, especially fast walking, four to five times a week.
3. A wise, close, personal, sharing friendship.
4. A change in your schedule that decreases your load—less activity.
5. When needed, professional counseling. But try your pastor first. If there are reasons for professional counseling that are clearly visible, he can probably see them. Most pastors have some counseling knowledge and the price is always right.

   Whether you go to a pastor or a professional counselor, be willing to stop seeing him if he causes more anguish than he cures. Find someone else, but don't lose hope. Your situation is not hopeless! Don't let the enemy lie to you and tell you that it is. If you trust God, at His appointed time He will lift you up again. Remind yourself, "I can do all things in him [Christ] who strengthens me" (Philippians 4:13).

Building a Support Group

"How do I put together a support group?"

Before developing one of your own, look around a bit. There may be one close by. Start by calling large churches nearby. (Be sure they hold a strong commitment to the Bible as God's Word.) If they don't have a support group ask them if they know of any. Assistant pastors (and their secretaries) are often more aware of support ministries, so I suggest you to talk to one of them.

If you can't find a group elsewhere, ask your pastor for permission to begin one. Search out an older, godly couple with a heart for hurting people, and ask them if they will help. Advertise in church newsletters, announcing that anyone interested in a singles' fellowship should come to a planning meeting on a certain date. Meet in a home, and eat together every time you meet.

If your group begins with the newly-wounded, design your meetings to deal with topics that promote healing. Jim Smoke's book *Growing Through Divorce* (Harvest House) is an excellent one to begin with. Read a chapter a week and discuss it. Let the older couple guide the meetings.

Set aside time to share your deepest hurts and pray for one another. Exchange phone numbers and call each other during the week for encouragement. Go to dinners and films, rent videos and watch them together and have game nights. Only a complete lack of imagination will keep you from growing. Just keep a healthy balance between serious and playful. The single-parent lifestyle is serious enough without working at making it so. Let everybody do something to help. That way each person is sharing in the success of the group.

Discovering a Place in the World

"How do you deal with divorcés feeling out of place or 'second class' in a couple-oriented society?"

Today there are slightly more divorces than marriages, and failed marriages are expected to increase during the next few years at an alarming rate. The only good thing about this tragedy is that it will cause the divorced person to feel less out of place.

Divorce carries with it a nagging sense of failure. No one (except the occasional sociopath!) gets through a divorce feeling altogether good about it. It is one of those things that only time can heal. As months and years go by, two things usually happen that help: You surround yourself with single friends; and the pain of the failure diminishes, eventually becoming a dull ache, recurring only now and then.

Society usually breaks down into homogeneous groups—groups that blend well. Democrat and Republican. Blue-collar and white-collar. Young and old. Liberal and conservative. If you are single again, surround yourself with single friends and you will immediately recognize a feeling of equality. Remember, anyone you meet may be part of a failure. Certainly not all the married people you know are successfully or happily married. Haven't you noticed?

Coping with Sexuality

"How do you make it without sex?
How do you stay moral?"

My dad used to say, "Son, keep your pants on and your zipper up and you won't make me a young grandfather." It was his way of saying, "Don't get into the situation and you won't have the problem."

Everyone who becomes single again must answer the question, "Who do I want to please with my life?" If you are convinced that you have a right to happiness on your own terms, you'll be in bed with someone as soon as you can get there.

Each Christian, single or married, must understand that one of the Bible's most clearly-stated doctrines is no sex outside the bonds of marriage. There is no way around it, under it or over it. It is clear as a bell.

Pleasing God means being abstinent unless you are married. For those people who had very satisfying sex lives, this abstinence can be as excruciating as giving up smoking or drugs.

The rules didn't change while you were married, and haven't for thousands of years. God didn't give His commandment in order to frustrate humanity. He made rules so that there would be something special, something wonderfully unique about marriage. Sex is part of the glue that holds a marriage together, and we only have so much glue. When we spread it all around, there doesn't seem to be enough to keep a new marriage together. Sex is God's bonding agent. Isn't it odd that when we say "He was unfaithful to his marriage," we are only talking about one thing?

That doesn't mean George didn't take out the garbage weekly. It means George (or Georgia!) had sexual relations with someone besides his mate. God has reserved exclusive sexuality as the badge of faithfulness. When a person is unfaithful, the marriage has only a 15 percent chance of lasting. Sex is like a diamond, meant to be worn only for one formal occasion—the occasion of marriage. It is not like a baseball to be thrown around to everyone. It is a gift to be given to the king or the queen, saved for the most special of relationships—marriage.

As a pastor, I can tell you this with confidence. If you are promiscuous, you will wish you hadn't been. You may think that an intimate moment will make you happy, but it doesn't. It makes you empty. It makes you feel used and like a user. It brings guilt, not pride, and fills your cup with vanity, not joy.

I have heard a hundred confessions of empty, miserable people who were sexually active before their wedding day. I have yet to hear one person come forward and tell me, "You're crazy! I've found out that sex apart from marriage is great!"

It's up to you. Do anything you have to do to stay out of bed before your next marriage. It *is* difficult. But I am confident God will bless you greatly if you obey Him in this way.

Building Relationships

"How do you deal with loneliness?"

As mentioned before, "Isolation is devastation. Involvement is the answer." The very first assessment that God made concerning the human personality was "It is not good that man should be alone." Knowing that God considers it unfavorable to be alone, it is worth every effort to make new friendships or cultivate old ones once you find yourself in the single-parent lifestyle.

So often we expect to be somehow rescued from our loneliness. That can be like waiting for a bus on a corner where buses never stop anymore. Most people these days operate on a "don't get involved" basis. And the rapid movement of our society has everyone too busy to notice needs. That means you'll have to make some moves yourself!

For immediate needs, your own family can be of help. Spending time with the people who have known you the longest can help you feel that some things do last and have substance. Chances are, however, that you won't feel as comfortable with your married friends as you once did. They may tend to remind you that you are, indeed, alone. I have heard hundreds of single parents say that, since the divorce, they feel odd and out of place with married people. This is not always the case, but is usually so.

What does this mean? It simply indicates that you will have to journey through space and time to a place where few enjoy being—*The Discomfort Zone*. That means you are about to go through the process of making a new set of friends. It's time for you to make the decision that you will not spend one more lonely week. Look through your personal phone directory, call up some old friends and begin a search for new ones.

Single-parent groups are springing up all over the United States and Canada. Churches are starting them at a phenomenal rate. Get on the phone and begin your search! As I mentioned before, large churches usually have the resources to put groups like this together, or at least will know where they exist. I would begin there.

Community groups are also forming all over. Although I prefer the Church as a meeting place for Christians who are going through dark valleys, I think secular groups can be wonderful. You must realize that you are very vulnerable, but if you set healthy boundaries for your life you will do fine.

You may want to start a group in your home and do things together. Remember, it only takes two to be company. Even if you invite just one other person to join you, go to dinner, a show or a church activity and enjoy yourselves.

There are thousands of people like you. Remember, Thoreau said, "Most people live lives of quiet desperation." The great sadness is that it is all so unnecessary. It's really a matter of getting up, getting out and getting going.

If you live alone in a residence where you can have a pet, consider the fact that they make great company. Dogs, cats and birds do not monopolize the conversation. They love to be near you. They agree with everything you say (except for some cats). They accept you for who you are and are often very affectionate. They do occasionally wet the rug, but nobody's perfect.

I have a low tolerance level for loneliness. I can get lonely driving to work, and it's only a 15-minute drive! Sometimes I wonder what kind of basket case I would be if Carol died or left me.

I began a good habit 14 years ago when I read a small book, *Confessions of a Christian Mystic,* which encouraged the reader to develop "God consciousness"—an awareness that God is there. He is with you, next to you, in you, all the time. I decided to practice that, and it worked. Nowadays, I sense God's presence all the time, and our relationship is very conversational.

I am only alone when I forget that God is near, or when we are not on speaking terms because I am ashamed of myself. Jesus is the friend that sticks closer than a brother. What a friend we have in Jesus!

Exploring Possible Abuse

*"What steps do I take
if I think that my children are
being abused when they
visit my ex?"*

If you have a lawyer, call him and get some legal advice. If you don't have an attorney, find a good one. Local child protection agencies may react differently to abuse accusations from one state to another. Your lawyer will know your local situation.

Proving child abuse is not a simple matter. Consider this possibility: Suppose your children do show evidence of abuse, but will not, for their own reasons, incriminate your ex. You may become suspect! If so, your children will be removed from your home until the culprit can be determined. Many times ex-spouses are accused unjustly during custody battles. Judges are at a loss to do anything unless they have hard evidence. Almost every person who is licensed by the state is required to report child abuse. That includes teachers, doctors and therapists.

You had better be prepared to prove your suspicions before you make too much of them. If you try and fail the first time, proof will become more and more difficult to get in the future. You cannot withhold visitation when the court has established it. So whatever you do, don't refuse to let the children visit your ex, or you may be found in contempt of court. These are the reasons that you should call your lawyer the instant you suspect abuse but cannot prove it.

If you can prove abuse, move as quickly as possible to prevent it from happening again. You might even want to call your local child protection agency yourself. Do not be surprised if your claims are met with some skepticism. Agencies get this kind of accusation all the time. Divorcing parents sometimes make these accusations for vindictive reasons

Collecting Child Support

"What do I do about late child support?"

If this is a chronic problem and you want to avoid the hassle of arguing with your ex, contact your state authorities. More and more states are willing to attach paychecks and garnish wages to ensure that mothers are well protected.

Before you go for the throat though, you may want to get an accurate picture of why your former spouse is unable to pay. There could be extenuating circumstances. It might be to your benefit to wait. Let's say that your husband is a salesman or a commuter who depends on his automobile for work. He blows an engine and uses a paycheck to handle the bill. This puts him a month behind, but still allows him to generate an income. In this kind of situation, you might be wise to allow a grace period.

In the case of blatant irresponsibility, your first call should be to the district attorney's office or whatever agency in your state enforces child and spousal support. They should be able to help you, and you should not need to retain a lawyer.

Evaluating Self-Esteem

"How important is self-esteem?"

The Bible doesn't teach self-love, but assumes it. It tells us "No man hates his own flesh but nourishes it and cherishes it." It tells us to love our neighbor as we love ourselves. The assumption is that we do love ourselves, since that is the established basis for how we are to love other people. What Scripture teaches clearly is self-denial. Forget yourself and allow God to take care of you. Trust Him for your care.

I am the most thankful pastor in the world. I have a group full of members who are poor in spirit. Because of that, anyone can walk through our door and be welcomed. There is no sense of superiority. My people see themselves as failures, so they are ready to learn and their hands are open to what God can give them.

Humility is a prized character quality and the divorced nearly always receive it as a gift for going through the process. Isaiah speaks for God when he says, "This is the man to whom I will look, he that is humble and contrite in spirit, and trembles at my word" (Isaiah 66:2).

God spent 40 years taking the self-esteem out of His servant Moses so He could use him. If you feel like you have lost it, please don't waste any time looking for it. Let it go and let Christ become your sufficiency. It is from Him that our true worth should originate.

You and I have value because Christ died for us. We have power because His Spirit is in us. We are clean because He has forgiven us. How can we be proud when He did all the work? No! Self-esteem is not only unimportant, it is dangerous. Best of all, give me a person who doesn't worry about his shortcomings *nor* revel in his gifts. Give me a person who doesn't think about himself much at all. Because when everything is said and done, trusting Christ is preferable to trusting self.

Growing in the Spirit

---

*"How do we nurture
our spiritual lives while going through
this period of being single parents?"*

There is no doubt in my mind that single parents, especially custodial ones, have the least free or optional time of any subculture I know. That makes it an ever greater wonder when I see our single parents so busy helping others. Where do they find the time?

I am convinced that nobody *has* time for one thing or another. People *make* time, and they especially make time for the things they value most. Spiritual nurture should be the most highly valued of all because it imparts strength, brings peace, offers hope and provides answers to the deepest questions of the soul.

Time spent in the presence of God provides you with the spiritual road map you need. Without it, you won't know where you're going or how to get there. The components of growth in the Lord are well-known. But, in case you are new to this sort of thing, let's review them.

A. *Worship and Praise.* Every Sunday, God's people worship Him. They gather to sing, praise and give of their substance. It is clear that there is something sacred and different about the Sabbath. It is included in God's top ten concerns for our behavior. "Remember the sabbath day to keep it holy" (Exodus 20:8). When you worship God, you fulfill the purpose for which you were created.

There are two important things to remember, however. God will not receive our worship if we are living in disobedience to His will; and the Sabbath, though it is reserved for worship, is not the only appropriate time to honor God. Anytime worship occurs to you is appropriate, because God is always worthy of our praise and adoration.

B. *Prayer is essential to spiritual nurture.* Whether formal or informal or private, prayer is our link to God. Prayer can take several forms. We can tell God how wonderful He is—that is praise. In obedience to His Word, we can confess to Him those things that we have done wrong and ask His forgiveness—that is confession. We can expectantly ask for things for ourselves and for our children, families and friends, if the things we ask for are in God's will—that is intercession. All prayer has a common purpose, however. It brings us into the presence of God, where there is peace and joy and blessing.

C. *Bible Study is indispensable.* The Bible tells us that faith comes by hearing, and hearing by the Word of God. Some portions of Scripture may not make any sense to you without the help of a biblical instructor.

Find a teacher that you respect and listen to him. As you grow, spend more and more time reading the Bible by yourself. The principles of the Bible can be understood by everyone, with God's Spirit as a guide.

Christian radio stations are terrific for Bible study, but be careful. There are some real nuts out there, anxious to get your money. Find good speakers like Chuck Swindoll, Jim Dobson and Rich Buhler. Stay away from legalistic and narrow teachers who have a sure-fire formula for everything. You'll notice that they harp on one theme all the time, and beg and grovel for your money. (Don't hesitate to help support those with valuable ministries, by the way.) Radio Bible study is great for single parents because you can do other things while you listen.

D. *Christian Fellowship is vital to spiritual growth.* If you desire to grow, you need to spend time with other Christians. The Bible says, "We know that we have passed out of death into life, because we love the brethren" (1 John 3:14).

Christians have two families. One family raised us, and we are linked to them by physical birth. The other is our family of believers, those who share the same Heavenly Father and are one with us in Christ. God has designed us for fellowship—with Him, and with other Christians.

Don't fail to reach out to each other!

———————

Now! Will you allow me one last word? Although you may ask all the right questions and memorize all the right answers, there is no magic formula for successful single parenting. And most assuredly, nothing can really help you deal with single parenthood's demands, hurts, obstacles and challenges unless you choose to be obedient to God's Word.

With all my heart, I appeal to you to wholeheartedly commit your past, your present and your future to the nail-scarred hands of the One who created you, died for you and lives to intercede for you.

Without Him, you can do nothing.

With Him, all things are possible!

APPENDICES

The Servant As a Forgiver

by Charles R. Swindoll

Forgiveness is not an elective in the curriculum of servanthood. It is a required course, and the exams are always tough to pass.

Several years ago I traveled to Trinity Evangelical Divinity School in search of a pastoral intern. In the process of interviewing a number of men, I met a seminarian I will never forget. As it turned out, I did not select him to come for the summer, but I was extremely impressed with his sensitivity to God. Although young and inexperienced, his spirit was tender and he spoke with gentleness. It was obvious that the Lord was deeply at work in his life. The marks of a servant's heart were clearly visible, so much so I probed to discover why. Among other things he related an incredible, true story that illustrated how God was molding him and shaping him through one of those tough "forgiveness exams." As best as I can remember, here's his story. I'll call him Aaron, not his real name.

Late one spring he was praying about having a signifi-cant ministry the following summer. He asked God for a position to open up on some church staff or Christian organization. Nothing happened. Summer arrived, still nothing. Days turned into weeks, and Aaron finally faced reality—he needed *any* job he could find. He checked the want ads and the only thing that seemed a possibility was driving a bus in southside Chicago... nothing to brag about, but it would help with tuition in the fall. After learning the route, he was on his own—a rookie driver in a dangerous section of the city. It wasn't long before Aaron realized just *how* dangerous his job really was.

A small gang of tough kids spotted the young driver, and began to take advantage of him. For several morn-ings in a row they got on, walked right past him without paying, ignored his warnings, and rode until they decided to get off... all the while making smart remarks to him and others on the bus. Finally, he decided that had gone on long enough.

The next morning, after the gang got on as usual, Aaron saw a policeman on the next corner, so he pulled over and reported the offense. The officer told them to pay or get off. They paid... but, unfortunately, the policeman got off. And *they* stayed on. When the bus turned another corner or two, the gang assaulted the young driver.

When he came to, blood was all over his shirt, two teeth were missing, both eyes were swollen, his money was gone, and the bus was empty. After returning to the terminal and being given the weekend off, our friend went to his little apartment, sank onto his bed and stared at the ceiling in disbelief. Resentful thoughts swarmed his mind. Confusion, anger, and disillusion-ment added fuel to the fire of his physical pain. He spent a fitful night wrestling with his Lord.

How can this be? Where's God in all of this?
I genuinely want to serve Him. I prayed for a

minstry. I was willing to serve Him anywhere, doing anything... and *this* is the thanks I get!

On Monday morning Aaron decided to press charges. With the help of the officer who had encountered the gang and several who were willing to testify as witnesses against the thugs, most of them were rounded up and taken to the local county jail. Within a few days there was a hearing before the judge.

In walked Aaron and his attorney plus the angry gang members who glared across the room in his direction. Suddenly he was seized with a whole new series of thoughts. Not bitter ones, but compassionate ones! His heart went out to the guys who had attacked him. Under the Spirit's control he no longer hated them—he pitied them. They needed help, not more hate. What could he do? Or say?

Suddenly, after there had been a plea of guilty, Aaron (to the surprise of his attorney and everybody else in the courtroom) stood to his feet and requested permission to speak.

Your honor, I would like you to total up all the days of punishment against these men— all the time sentenced against them—and I request that you allow me to go to jail in their place.

The judge didn't know whether to spit or wind his watch. Both attorneys were stunned. As Aaron looked over at the gang members (whose mouths and eyes looked like saucers), he smiled and said quietly, "It's because I forgive you."

The dumfounded judge, when he reached a level of composure, said rather firmly: "Young man, you're out of order. This sort of thing has never been done before!" To which the young man replied with genius insight:

> Oh, yes, it has, your honor...yes, it has. It
> happened over 19 centuries ago when a man
> from Galilee paid the penalty that all man-
> kind deserved.

And then, for the next three or four minutes, without interruption, he explained how Jesus Christ died on our behalf, thereby proving God's love and forgiveness.

He was not granted his request, but the young man visited the gang members in jail, led most of them to faith in Christ, and began a significant ministry to many others in southside Chicago.

He passed a tough exam. And, as a result, a large door of ministry—the very thing he'd prayed for—opened up before him. Through the pain of abuse and assault, Aaron began to get a handle on serving others.

Forgiving (like giving) improves our serve!

God's Forgiveness of Us

As we undertake a subject this broad, it's necessary that we limit our thoughts to horizontal forgiveness rather than vertical forgiveness. But instead of ignoring the vertical altogether, perhaps I should briefly explain its significance. Actually, it's God's forgiveness of us that makes possible our forgiving others.

When the penalty of our sin was paid in full by Jesus Christ on the cross, God's wrath was expressed against Him—the One who took our place. God was therefore satisfied in the epochal sacrifice...allowing all who would turn, in faith, to the Son of God to be totally, once-for-all, forgiven. Christ's blood washed away our sin. And from the moment we believe on Him, we stand forgiven, relieved of guilt, before a satisfied God, freeing Him to shower upon us His grace and love.

Remember the verse from that grand old song the church has sung for years?

My sin—oh, the bliss of this glorious tho't—
My sin—not in part, but the whole,
Is nailed to the cross and I bear it no more,
Praise the Lord, praise the lord, O my soul![1]

That says it well, but not as beautifully as the song
from the oldest of all hymnals—The Psalms:

Bless the Lord, O my soul;
And all that is within me, bless His holy
    name.
Bless the Lord, O my soul,
And forget none of His benefits;
    Who pardons all your iniquities;
Who heals all your diseases;
    Who redeems your life from the pit;
Who crowns you with lovingkindness and
    compassion;
    Who satisfies your years with good
        things,
So that your youth is renewed like the
    eagle....
    He has not dealt with us according to
    our sins,
Nor rewarded us according to our iniquities.
    For high as the heavens are above the
    earth,
So great is His loving kindness toward
    those who fear Him.
    As far as the east is from the west,
So far has He removed our transgressions
    from us
(Psalm 103:1-5,10-12).

That's what Aaron helped the Chicago gang to understand. They ultimately had little difficulty realizing

what Christ accomplished on the cross on their behalf. But what they did not understand at the time was that Aaron could never have done that for them, horizontally, if it had not been for what Christ had already done for Aaron, vertically. Not until we fully accept *and appropriate* God's infinite and complete forgiveness on our behalf can we carry out the things I mention in the rest of this chapter.

Our Forgiveness of One Another

It isn't long before anyone who gets serious about serving others must come to terms with forgiving others as well. Yes, *must*. As I said earlier, it's a required course in the servanthood curriculum. Since this is such a common occurrence, I find it helpful to break the subject down into manageable parts, with handles I can get hold of.

Only Two Possibilities

When wrong has been done against another person, there are only two possibilities. But whether we are responsible for the offense or are the recipients of it, the first move is always ours. The true servant doesn't keep score. The general principle is set forth in Ephesians 4:31-32, which says:

> Let all bitterness and wrath and anger and clamor and slander be put away from you, along with all malice.
> And be kind to one another, tender-hearted, forgiving each other, just as God in Christ also has forgiven you.

That's a beautiful summation of the whole subject of forgiveness. It describes how to live with a clear conscience and thus be free to serve. And observe the reminder—you forgive others "...as God in Christ also has forgiven you" (vertical). But we need to get more specific. Let's analyze both sides of the forgiveness coin.

When You Are the Offender

Matthew 5:23-24 describes, in a nutshell, the correct response and procedure to follow when we have been in the wrong and offended someone.

> If therefore you are presenting your offering at the altar, and there remember that your brother has something against you, leave your offering there before the altar, and go your way; first be reconciled to your brother, and then come and present your offering.

The scene is clear. A person in Jesus' day has come to worship. At that time, in keeping with the Jewish law and custom, worshipers brought sacrificial animals or birds with them. The sacrifice would be slain before God, providing cleansing of sin and a way of open access to prayer. Today it would simply be a Christian's coming to his Father in prayer. Either way, the worshiper is suddenly seized with the inescapable thought, the painful realization that he or she has offended another person. In the words of Jesus, you "...remember your brother has something against you." What do you do?

Stop! Don't ignore that realization. Don't just plunge on into prayer, even though that may be your first reaction. God wants us, rather, to be sensitive to His quiet prompting.

In verse 24, we are instructed to do four things:

1. Stop	"leave your offering there...."
2. Go	"go your way...."
3. Reconcile	"...first be reconciled. .."

| 4. Return | "... then come and present your offering...." |

The key term is *reconciled*. It's from a Greek root verb that means "to alter, to change"... with a prefix attached to the verb that means "through." In other words, we are commanded to go through a process that will result in a change. Clearly, the *offender* is to initiate the action.

One reliable authority defines this word rather vividly: "To change enmity for friendship...bringing about mutual concession for mutual hostility."[2] And another, "Seeing to it that the angry brother renounce his enmity...."[3]

That needs little clarification. We are to go (ideally, personally—if not possible, at least by phone or letter) and confess both the wrong and our grief over the offense, seeking the forgiveness of the one we wounded. *Then* we are free to return to God in worship and prayer.

"But what if he or she won't forgive?" Good question! The important thing for each of us to remember is that you are responsible for *you* and I am responsible for *me*. With the right motive, in the right spirit, at the right time, out of obedience to God, we are to humble ourselves (remember, it is servanthood we're developing) and attempt to make things right. God will honor our efforts. The one offended may need time—first to get over the shock and next, to have God bring about a change in his or her heart. Healing sometimes takes time. Occasionally, a lot of time.

"What if the situation only gets worse?" Another good question frequently asked. This can happen. You see, all the time the one offended has been blaming you...mentally sticking pins in your doll...thinking all kinds of bad things about you. When you go to make things right, you suddenly cause his internal scales to go out of balance. You take away the blame and all that's left is the person's guilt, which does a number on him, resulting in even worse feelings. But now it's no longer your fault. Illustration? King Saul and young David. In case you don't remember, young David became a threat to the paranoid monarch. No matter how hard he tried to win back the favor of Saul, things only got worse. It took *years* for the troubled king to realize that David was sincere in his efforts to make things right. Again, it may take awhile for God to get through.

"What if I decide to simply deal with it before God and not go through the hassle and embarrassment of talking with the other person?" We'll do *anything* to make things easier, won't we? Well, first off—that is a willful contradiction of the command. Jesus says, "Stop, go, reconcile, and return!" *Not* to go is direct disobedience. It also can result in things getting worse.

Let's say I am driving away from your church parking lot next Sunday morning. I back my car into the side of your beautiful, new *Mercedes 450 SEL*. CRUNCH! You are visiting with friends following the service and you hear the noise. Your stomach churns as you see me get out of the car, look at the damage... and then bow in prayer:

> Dear Lord, please forgive me for being so preoccupied and clumsy. And please give John grace as he sees the extensive damage I have caused out of sheer negligence. And provide his needs as he takes this car in to have it fixed. Thanks, Lord. Amen.

As I drive away, I wave and smile real big as I yell out the window, "It's all cleared up, John. I claimed the damage before God. *Isn't grace wonderful!*"

Tell me, how does that grab you? I have rather strong doubts that it would suddenly make things A-O.K., no matter how sincere my prayer might have been. You and I know that would do no good.

When I was a kid in church we used to sing a little chorus that sounded so pious, so right. In fact, we would often close our youth meetings by holding hands in a circle and sing this piece with our eyes closed:

> If I have wounded any soul today,
>   If I have caused one foot to go astray,
> If I have walked in my own willful way
>   Dear Lord, forgive![4]

I now question the message of that nice-sounding song. Wounded souls are offended people. And the Savior does not say, "Simply pray and I'll forgive you." In fact, He says, "Stop praying until you have made things right!" That is the part of the "forgiveness exam" that's tough to pass.

One final question before moving on to the other side of the coin: "What if it is impossible for me to reconcile because the offended person has died?" Obviously, you cannot contact the dead. It's impossible to get a hearing, but your conscience still badgers you. In such unique cases, I recommend that you share your burden of guilt with someone whom you can trust. A close friend, your mate, a counselor or your pastor. Be specific and completely candid. Pray with that individual and confess openly the wrong and the guilt of your soul. In such cases—and only in such cases—prayer and the presence of an understanding, affirming individual will provide the relief you need so desperately.

After David had indirectly murdered Uriah, Bathsheba's husband, his guilt was enormous. Adultery and hypocrisy on top of murder just about did him in. If you want to know the depth of his misery, read Psalm 32:3-4:

> When I kept silent about my sin, my body
>   wasted away
> Through my groaning all day long.

For day and night Thy hand was heavy upon
  me;
My vitality was drained away as with the
  fever-heat of summer.

Finally, when it all caved in on top of him, when he
broke the hypocritical silence and sought God's forgiveness, Uriah was not there to hear his confession. He had
been dead the better part of a year. But David was not
alone. A prophet named Nathan was there, you may
recall. And when the broken king poured out his soul, "I
have sinned...," Nathan followed quickly with these
affirming words: "The Lord also has taken away your
sin; you shall not die" (2 Samuel 12:13).

When you have been the cause of an offense, that is,
when you are the offender, have the heart of a servant.
Stop, go, reconcile, and then return.

When You Are the Offended

Turn now to Matthew 18:21-35... same book, same
teacher, similar subject, but a different style and setting
entirely from the Matthew 5 passage where Jesus delivered a monologue communicating a large number of
things to His disciples. He touched on each rather generally, all great truths... but many subjects. Here in
chapter 18 He is engaged in more of a dialogue, dealing
in depth with the right response toward someone who
offends us. Rather than dump the whole truckload on
you, let me present these verses in sections.

First, the disciple's question:

Then Peter came and said to Him, "Lord,
how often shall my brother sin against me and
I forgive him? Up to seven times?" (Matthew
18:21).

Good, relevant question. What's the limit we should place on forgiveness? Peter was feeling magnanimous that day, for the going rate (according to the rabbis) was three times.[5] The Jews were instructed to forgive once, forgive twice...and a third time, but from then on, forget it. Peter doubled the limit then added a bonus for good measure.

Now, the Lord's response:

> ...I do not say to you, up to seven times, but
> up to seventy times seven (Matthew 18:22).

Obviously, He is not saying literally, "Would you believe 490, Peter?" No, not that. He's suggesting an *infinite* number of times. *Limitless.* I would imagine that thought blew those disciples away! Which, no doubt, prompted Jesus to go into greater detail. Hence, a parable with a punch line. Read the story very carefully, preferably aloud and slowly.

> For this reason the kingdom of heaven may be compared to a certain king who wished to settle accounts with his slaves.
> And when he had begun to settle them, there was brought to him one who owed him ten thousand talents.
> But since he did not have the means to repay, his lord commanded him to be sold, along with his wife and children and all that he had, and repayment to be made.
> The slave therefore falling down, prostrated himself before him, saying, "Have patience with me, and I will repay you everything."
> And the lord of that slave felt compassion and released him and forgave him the debt.
> But that slave went out and found one of his fellow-slaves who owed him a hundred denarii; and he seized him and began to choke him, saying, "Pay back what you owe."

So his fellow-slave fell down and began to entreat him, saying, "Have patience with me and I will repay you."

He was unwilling however, but went and threw him in prison until he should pay back what was owed.

So when his fellow-slaves saw what had happened, they were deeply grieved and came and reported to their lord all that had happened.

Then summoning him, his lord said to him, "You wicked slave, I forgave you all that debt because you entreated me.

"Should you not also have had mercy on your fellow-slave, even as I had mercy on you?"

And his lord, moved with anger, handed him over to the torturers until he should repay all that was owed him (Matthew 18:23-34).

By now, you have probably begun to think in terms of vertical forgiveness and horizontal forgiveness. The vertical is clearly seen in verses 23 through 27. This was an incredible debt (about $10,000,000!) requiring infinite forgiveness, which the king provided (read verse 27 again)—a beautiful reminder of God's forgiving the sinner.

The horizontal comes in view in verses 28 through 34. That same slave, having just been forgiven that incredible debt, turned against a fellow who owed him *less than twenty bucks* and assaulted the poor fellow. When the king got word of his violent reaction, he was furious. I mean, he was beside himself! And the confrontation that followed was understandably severe.

A couple of things emerge from the latter part of this story that provide us with reasons to forgive others.

1. To refuse to forgive is hypocritical. Note again verses 32 through 33.

Then summoning him, his lord said to him, "You wicked slave, I forgave you all that debt because you entreated me.

"Should you not also have had mercy on your fellow-slave, even as I had mercy on you?"

Since we have been the recipients of maximum mercy, who are we to suddenly demand justice from others? The compassion [that] God (illustrated in the parable as the king) demonstrates on our behalf calls for us to do the same toward others. Anything less is downright hypocritical.

2. To refuse to forgive inflicts inner torment upon us. Remember how the story ends? It is exceedingly significant. "And his lord, moved with anger, handed him over to the torturers until he should repay all that was owed him."

"Well," you say, "that was just a parable. We can't press every point and say each little detail applies to us." Granted, but in this case, it's not a *little* detail. It's the punch line, the climax of the whole story. How can I say that? Because verse 35 is not part of the parable. It is a statement Jesus makes *after* the story ends. It is His penetrating application of the whole parable on forgiving others.

He wrapped up His instruction with this grim warning: "So shall My Heavenly Father also do to you, if each of you does not forgive his brother from your heart."

Frankly, this is one of the most important truths God ever revealed to me on the consequences of an unforgiving spirit. When Jesus says, "So shall My heavenly Father also do to you...," He is referring back to the closing words of the parable, which says:

And his lord, moved with anger, handed him over to the torturers until he should repay all that was owed him.

This is no fictitious tale, like Bluebeard who tortured others behind a secret door. No, Jesus says God personally will allow those who refuse to forgive others to be tortured.

What in the world does that mean? The root Greek term from which "torturers" is translated is a verb meaning "to torment"—a frightening thought. When I first saw the thing begin to take shape in my mind, I resisted it. I thought, "No, that's too harsh!" But the further I probed, the clearer it became.

The same term is used to describe a person suffering "great pain" (Matthew 8:6). And it is used to describe the misery of a man being "in agony" in hell as he pleads for relief (Luke 16:23-24). When we read of a man named Lot, in 2 Peter 2:8, who was surrounded and oppressed by the conduct of unprincipled men, we read "his righteous soul was tormented day after day...." Again the same term is used. Pain, agony and torment are all a part of this torturous experience.

But here in Matthew 18:34-35, Jesus refers to tormentors—a noun, not a verb. He is saying the one who refuses to forgive, the Christian who harbors grudges, bitter feelings toward another, will be turned over to torturous thoughts, feelings of misery, and agonizing unrest within. One fine expositor describes it like this:

> This is a marvelously expressive phrase to describe what happens to us when we do not forgive another. It is an accurate description of gnawing resentment and bitterness, the awful gall of hate or envy. It is a terrible feeling. We cannot get away from it. We feel strongly this separation from another and every time we think of them we feel within the acid of resentment and hate eating away at our peace and calmness. This is the torturing that our Lord says will take place.[6]

218

And who hasn't endured such feelings? It is one of the horrible consequences of *not* forgiving those who offend us. It makes no difference who it is—one of your parents or in-laws, your pastor or former pastor, a close friend who turned against you, some teacher who was unfair, or a business partner who ripped you off...even your former partner in marriage. I meet many divorcées who have been "handed over to the torturers" for this very reason. Believe me, it is not worth the misery. We are to forgive as we have been forgiven! Release the poison of all that bitterness...let it gush out before God, and declare the sincere desire to be free. It's one of the major steps each of us must take toward becoming God's model of a servant.

How to Make It Happen

There is enough in this chapter to keep us thinking (and forgiving) for weeks. But there are a couple of specifics that need to be considered before we move ahead.

First, *focus fully on God's forgiveness of you.* Don't hurry through this. Think of how vast, how extensive His mercy has been extended toward you. Like Aaron, the young seminary student, must have done in the courtroom that day. Like David did when he wrote, "Hymn 103." He got extremely specific. Remember?

> Bless the Lord, O my soul,
>   And forget none of His benefits;
> Who pardons all your iniquities;
>   Who heals all your diseases;
> Who redeems your life from the pit;
>   Who crowns you with lovingkindness and
>   compassion;
> Who satisfies your years with good things,
>   So that your youth is renewed like the
>   eagle

He has not dealt with us according to our sins,
Nor rewarded us according to our inquities.
For high as the heavens are above the earth,
So great is His lovingkindness toward
those who fear Him.
As far as the east is from the west,
So far has He removed our transgressions
from us
(Psalm 103:2-5,10-12).

Meditate on that in your own life. Personalize these words by substituting *me* and *my* for *us* and *your*. Ponder the depth of God's mercy...the debts against you He graciously canceled. The extent to which you can envision God's forgiveness of you, to that same measure you will be given the capacity to forgive others.

Next, *deal directly and honestly with any resentment you currently hold against anyone.*

It's a tough exam. But think of the alternative—torturing, agonizing feelings, the churning within, the enormous emotional energy you burn up and waste every day.

Maybe you are willing to go just so far. You will bargain with God and agree to forgive *but* not *forget*. That is one of the most regrettable mistakes a servant-in-the-making can make. Because limited forgiveness is like conditional love—a poor substitute for the genuine item. It's no forgiveness at all.

Amy Carmichael said it best when she wrote these words.

If I say, "Yes, I forgive, but I cannot forget,"
as though the God, who twice a day washes all
the sands on all the shores of all the world,
could not wash such memories from my mind,
then I know nothing of Calvary love.[7]

So much for forgiving. After forgiving we need to think about forgetting. If forgiveness is the process God takes us through to heal inner wounds... then forgetting would be the removal of the ugly scar.

And God can even do that.

Note: "The Servant As a Forgiver" was excerpted from Charles R. Swindoll, *Improving Your Serve* (Waco, TX: Word Books, 1981). Used by permission.

Notes

Chapter 3—Father to the Fatherless

1. Gary Smalley, morning message entitled "The Incredible Worth of a Woman," delivered July 1989 at the Forest Home Christian Conference Center.

Chapter 8—Wounded Lambs

1. Gary Richmond, *The Divorce Decision* (Waco, TX: Word Books, 1988), p. 31.
2. Ibid.
3. Bryce Christiansen, "Ties That Bind: Divorce and Teen Suicide," *Orange County Register* (Santa Ana, CA).

Chapter 9—Staying Tuned-In

1. Naomi Landorf has a Master of Science for Learning Handicapped, a Life Teaching Credential (Elementary), a Bachelor of Science (Psychology), a Resource Specialist Certification, and a Life Learning Handicapped Life credential. She currently lives in Upland, CA.

Chapter 10—Ready to Move On

1. Richmond, *The Divorce Decision.*
2. Pamela King, "Living Together: Bad for the Kids," *Psychology Today,* March 1989, p. 76.

Chapter 11—The Winner's Heart

1. Charles R. Swindoll, *Strengthening Your Grip* (Waco, TX: Word Books, 1982), p. 207.
2. Mary Campo is your basic single parent. She does child care in her home. She spoke to our group, Single Parent Fellowship on April 9, 1989. Her testimony is also printed in the Single Parent Fellowship Newsletter, Vol. 1, No. 2.
3. E. Lorraine Austin is a Bible teacher at La Crescenta First Baptist Church, La Crescenta, CA. She has taught Bible for 30 years and is one of my mentors.

Appendices—The Servant As a Forgiver

1. Horatio G. Spafford, "It Is Well with My Soul," copyright 1918 The John Church Co. Used by permission of the publisher.
2. G. Abbott-Smith, *A Manual Greek Lexicon of the New Testament* (Edinburgh: T. & T. Clark, 1921), p. 109.
3. G. Kittle, ed., *Theological Dictionary of the New Testament,* vol. 1 (Grand Rapids: Wm. B. Eerdmans Publishing Co., 1964), p. 253.
4. C. M. Battersby, "An Evening Prayer," copyright 1911 by Charles H. Gabriel. © renewed 1939, The Rodeheaver Co. (a div. of Word, Inc.). Used by permission.
5. Charles Caldwell Ryrie, *The Ryrie Study Bible: The New Testament* (Chicago: Moody Press, 1977), p. 56.
6. Ray C. Stedman, "Breaking the Resentment Barrier" (sermon delivered to Peninsula Bible Church, Palo Alto, CA, *Treasures of the Parable* Series, Message 11, July 13, 1969), p. 6.
7. Amy Carmichael, taken from *If,* copyrighted material, p. 48. Used by permission of the Christian Literature Crusade, Fort Washington, PA 19034.

Bibliography

The Single Parent Book Shelf

The following list of books is a place for you to start looking for more specific and in-depth answers to the questions with which you find yourself confronted if you are a single parent. The list was solicited from five sources: The pastors on the staff of First Evangelical Free Church of Fullerton, professional licensed marriage and family counselors, administrators and staff of a well-known chain of Christian bookstores, the counseling staff of Chuck Swindoll's radio broadcast "Insight for Living," and books recommended by Dr. James Dobson's "Focus on the Family" counseling staff.

Let me tell you the obvious. None of the contributors to this booklist would agree with all of the things written in all the books. You must be the one to determine what you will take and leave when you let an author into your mind. There is something helpful in every book on the list and that is what you should look for.

The list is by topic. Read four or five pages before you buy the books to make sure the author is readable for you. None of the books are divinely inspired though many of the authors are anointed by God to write. Nothing they say is worth anything if it contradicts the Bible.

Abortion

Stanford, Susan M. *Will I Cry Tomorrow?* Old Tappan, NJ: Fleming H. Revell, 1986.

Filled with despair resulting from an abortion, Stanford turned to the Lord and was restored. Now she helps other people who have had an abortion.

Abusive Behavior

Koone, Carolyn. *Beyond Betrayal: Healing My Broken Past.* New York: Harper and Row Publishers, Inc., 1986.

Koone shares her account of the process she went through to heal her painful memories.

Martin, Grant. *Please Don't Hurt Me.* Wheaton, IL: Victor Books, 1987.

A clinical psychologist's view of the abuse of children and spouses based on his patients' experiences.

Adultery

Dobson, Dr. James. *Love Must Be Tough: New Hope for Families in Crisis.* Waco, TX: Word, Inc., 1983.

Passive people have trouble standing up for themselves, and are often put in a position where they are manipulated and abused. Dobson explains how to take firm charge of your own life.

Affirmation

Smalley, Gary and Trent, John. *The Blessing.* Nashville: Thomas Nelson Publishers, 1986.

A description of the biblical history of parental blessings and the part they play in building a child's self-image.

Agoraphobia (fear of being in public places)

Weakes, Claire. *Peace from Nervous Suffering.* New York: Bantam Books, Inc., 1972

Dr. Weakes is an expert in the treatment of agoraphobia and gives counsel that will help people become confident and less nervous about going out in public.

Alcohol, Drug, and Substance Abuse

Campbell, Ross and Likes, Pat. *Your Child and Drugs: Help for Concerned Parents.* Wheaton, IL: Victor Books, 1988.
Dr. Campbell gives parents practical guidelines on helping their child overcome a substance abuse problem—covering the spiritual and emotional facets of addiction as well.

W., Claire. *God, Help Me Stop! Break Free from Addiction and Compulsion.* San Diego, CA: Books West CA, 1982.
A spiritual look at the Twelve Steps of the Alcoholics Anonymous program.

Assurance

Kendall, R.T. *Once Saved, Always Saved.* Chicago, IL: Moody Press, 1985.
A comfort-producing, comprehensive look at the issue of whether a believer can lose his salvation.

Bereavement

Barber, Cyril J. and Aspenlaitor, Sharalee. *Through the Valley of Tears.* Old Tappan, NJ: Fleming H. Revell, 1987.
Seeking to help children and adults who are suffering bereavement, this book walks through the Psalms, paralleling the natural steps of loss.

Children

Campbell, Ross. *How to Really Love Your Child.* Wheaton, IL: Victor Books, 1982.
Most of us at least know we were loved as children, though few of us *felt* loved. Learn how to make your children *feel* loved

Campbell, Ross. *How to Really Love Your Teenager.* Wheaton, IL: Victor Books, 1982.

Dobson, Dr. James. *Parenting Isn't for Cowards.* Waco, TX: Word, Inc., 1987.

Dobson, Dr. James. *Preparing for Adolescence.* Oxnard, CA: Vision House, 1980.
Pointed and practical, Dobson gives great counsel for those who never received it from their parents—especially the area of sexuality.

Swindoll, Charles R. *Growing Wise in Family Life.* Portland, OR: Multnomah Press, 1988.
A combination of biblical and personal wisdom on building a healthy family.

Swindoll, Charles R. *You and Your Child.* New York: Bantam Books, Inc., 1984.

Ziglar, Zig. *Raising Positive Kids in a Negative World.* Nashville, TN: Oliver-Nelson, 1985.

Codependency

Beattie, Melody. *Codependent No More: How to Stop Controlling Others and Start Caring for Yourself.* New York: Harper and Row Publishers, Inc., 1987.
An excellent book that explores the dynamics of dysfunctional relationships and the part that the "normal" partner may be playing to keep the dysfunction going.

Communication

Augsburger, David. *Caring Enough to Confront.* Ventura, CA: Regal Books, 1980.
This book is part of a great series on communication.

Jourard, Sidney. *The Transparent Self.* New York: Van Nostrand Reinhold Co., Inc., 1971.
Read with discernment, *The Transparent Self* will be very beneficial.

Smalley, Gary and Scott, Steve. *For Better or for Best.* Grand Rapids, MI: Zondervan Publishing House, 1982.

Smalley, Gary and Scott, Steve. *If He Only He Knew: A Valuable Guide to Knowing, Understanding, and Loving Your Wife.* Grand Rapids, MI: Zondervan Publishing House, 1982.

Smalley, Gary and Trent, John. *Language of Love: A Powerful Way to Maximize Insight, Intimacy and Understanding.* Pomona, CA: Focus on the Family Publishers, 1988.

Smalley, Gary and Trent, John. *The Gift of Honor.* Nashville, TN: Thomas Nelson Publishers, 1987.
An excellent book on how to communicate with your kids.

Wright, H. Norman. *Communication: Key to Your Marriage.* Ventura, CA: Regal Books, 1974.

Wright offers practical suggestions and guidelines to improve communication in marriage.

Dating

Hugget, Joyce. *Dating, Sex, and Friendship: An Open and Honest Guide to Healthy Relationships.* Downers Grove, IL: InterVarsity Press, 1985.
A veritable encyclopedia of biblical advice and insight on the tough issues surrounding dating.

Timmons, Tim and Hedges, Charlie. *Call It Love or Call It Quits.* Waco, TX: Word, Inc., 1988.
A guidebook for singles who find themselves falling into the dating pitfalls of either quick intimacy or hesitancy in making a commitment.

Depression

Ketterman, Grace. *Depression Hits Every Family.* Nashville, TN: Thomas Nelson Publishers, 1988.
Dr. Ketterman deals in a practical, yet warm way with depression.

Divorce

Sanderson, Carole. *Finding Your Place After Divorce: How Women*

Can Find Healing. Grand Rapids, MI: Zondervan Publishing House, 1986.
Sanderson focuses on the specific feelings and loss of hope that women face and provides help on combating them.

Emotional Healing

Backus, John and Chapian, Marie. *Telling Yourself the Truth*. Minneapolis, MN: Bethany House Publishers, 1980.
Straightforward, workable material on how to control your emotions.

Bradshaw, John. *Healing the Shame that Binds You*. Deerfield Beach, FL: Health Communications, Inc., 1988.
A secular work that emphasizes the invisible influences that operate in many Christians' backgrounds.

Buhler, Rich. *Pain and Pretending*. Nashville, TN: Thomas Nelson Publishers, 1988.

Lloyd-Jones, David Martyn. *Spiritual Depression*. Grand Rapids, MI: William B. Eerdmans Publishing Co., 1965.
Biblical talks that present a realistic view of faith.

Seamands, David. *Healing for Damaged Emotions*. Wheaton, IL: Victor Books, 1981.
An up-front and honest look at emotional healing.

Seamands, David. *Healing Grace: Let God Free You from the Performance Trap*. Wheaton, IL: Victor Books, 1988.
Seamands elaborates on how the grace of God can help us transform our hurtful memories and help change our hurtful behaviors.

Seamands, David. *Healing of Memories*. Wheaton, IL: Victor Books, 1985.
In this sequel to *Healing for Damaged Emotions,* Seamands describes how hurting people can find restoration through Christ.

Employment

Mattson, Ralph and Miller, Arthur. *Finding a Job You Can Love*. Nashville, TN: Thomas Nelson Publishers, 1982.

God created each person for a specific job. Mattson and Miller discuss how to find and then receive joy from that job.

Failure

Lutzer, Erwin W. *Failure: The Back Door to Success.* Chicago, IL: Moody Press, 1975.

Swindoll, Charles R. *Starting Over: Fresh Hope for the Road Ahead.* Portland, OR: Multnomah Press, 1977.
Stories that encourage down-and-out people to start over again.

Finance

Any book by Ron Blue or Larry Burkett will be beneficial. Each of them has individual books that deal with various topics. Check your local bookstore.

Friendship

Inrig, Gary. *Quality Friendship: The Risks and Rewards.* Chicago: Moody Press, 1981.
An in-depth exploration into high-quality friendships, with instructions on how to develop and maintain them.

Lifestyle, Developing a Healthy

Berry, Carman R. *When Helping You Is Hurting Me: Escaping the Messiah Trap.* New York: Harper and Row Publishers, Inc., 1989.
Some of us get so caught up in taking care of other people that we fail to take care of ourselves.

Finzel, Hans. *Help! I'm a Baby Boomer!* Wheaton, IL: Victor Books, 1989.

Hansel, Tim. *Holy Sweat: The Remarkable Things Ordinary People Can Do.* Waco, TX: Word, Inc., 1987.

Stott, John. *Your Mind Matters.* Downers Grove, IL: InterVarsity Press, 1973.
Stott helps us discover the importance of healthy thinking.

Loneliness

Elliot, Elizabeth. *Loneliness*. Nashville, TN: Thomas Nelson Publishers, 1988.
Mrs. Elliott, writing from personal experience, explains how a strong relationship with God will diminish the ache of loneliness.

Marriage

Joy, Donald M. *Rebonding: Preventing and Restoring Damaged Relationships*. Waco, TX: Word Books, 1986.
An explanation of how to restore broken or damaged interpersonal relationships.

Williams, Pat and Jill. *Rekindled: How to Keep the Warmth in Marriage*. Old Tappan, NJ: Fleming H. Revell Co., 1985.

Morality

Barclay, William. *Christian Ethics for Today*. New York: Harper and Row Publishers, Inc., 1984.
A hard-hitting description of the world as it is and how to deal with its ethics.

Coleman, Barry, ed. *Sex and the Single Christian: Candid Conversations*.Ventura, CA: Regal Books, 1986.

Penner, Cliff and Joyce. *The Gift of Sex*. Waco, TX: Word, Inc., 1981.

Sanders, J. Oswald. *Spiritual Leadership*. Chicago, IL: Moody Press, 1986.
Sanders comprehensively covers the topic of discipleship, including: your walk with Christ; involvement in the world; and leadership in the home, which is really a mini-church within four walls.

Motivation

Smalley, Gary. *The Key to Your Child's Heart*. Nashville, TN: Thomas Nelson Publishers, 1988.

After focusing on parenting mistakes, Smalley describes how to build a strong relationship with your child.

Remarriage

Frydenger, Tom and Frydenger, Adrienne. *The Blended Family.* Grand Rapids, MI: Zondervan, 1985.

Hart, Archibald D. *Children and Divorce.* Waco, TX: Word, Inc., 1982.
Hart helps parents learn to deal with the struggles facing children of divorced parents.

Swindoll, Charles R. *Strike the Original Match: Rekindling and Preserving Your Marriage Fire.* Portland, OR: Multnomah Press, 1980.
A biblical and practical look at God's rich and meaningful purpose for marriage.

Talley, Jim and Reed, Bobbie. *Too Close, Too Soon.* Nashville, TN: Thomas Nelson Publishers, 1982.
Though not written specifically for second marriages, this book has a lot of great material for older couples contemplating a second marriage.

Resentment, Overcoming

Augsburger, David. *Caring Enough to Forgive: Caring Enough Not to Forgive.* Ventura, CA: Regal Books, 1981.
Augsburger describes the necessity and the mechanics of forgiving.

Separation

Chapman, Gary. *Hope for the Separated: Wounded Marriages Can Be Healed.* Chicago, IL: Moody Press, 1982.
Focusing on torn feelings, Chapman teaches separated marriage partners to trust and care for each other. He also includes an honest look at issues facing people in the midst of marital separations.

Sexual Problems

Baker, Don. *Beyond Rejection: The Church, Homosexuality, and Hope*. Portland, OR: Multnomah Press, 1985.
Looking at the issue of homosexuality, Don Baker focuses on one couple, leaders in the church, who struggled with the husband's secret homosexuality.

White, John. *Eros Defiled: The Christian and Sexual Sin*. Downers Grove, IL: InterVarsity Press, 1977.
Dr. White examines the influence of the media and educational opinions of human sexuality on the Christian and counter-balances them with a biblical view of the role of sex in a Christian's life.

Spiritual Life

Bunyan, John. *Pilgrim's Progress*.
A Christian classic. Part II is the story of a single mother, Christiana, keeping her family on the road to heaven.

Crabb, Larry. *Inside Out*. Colorado Springs, CO: Navpress, 1988.
A look at the seeming paradoxes that Christians face in their spiritual lives: Why does the Christian life seem empty? Why is it difficult to obey God?

Family Walk (for children), *Youth Today* (for teenagers). Pomona, CA: Focus on the Family and Walk Thru the Bible Ministries.
Simple, daily, fun, and full of great suggestions.

Peterson, Eugene. *Traveling Light: Modern Meditations on St. Paul's Letter of Freedom*. Colorado Springs, CO: Helmers and Howard Publishers, Inc., 1988.
Christians can be free—free from the guilt people suffer from thinking that they're still under the burden of the law. Learn how to be free in Christ.

Swindoll, Charles R. *Growing Strong in the Seasons of Life*. Portland, OR: Multnomah Press, 1983.

Swindoll, Charles R. *Improving Your Serve*. Waco, TX: Word, Inc., 1981.

Tozer, A.W., comp. *The Christian Book of Mystical Verse.* Camp Hill, PA: Christian Publications, Inc., 1975.

A very moving book of poetry, songs, and hymns of the faith since the first century.

Tozer, A.W. *Knowledge of the Holy.* New York: Harper and Row Publishers, Inc., 1978.

This was one of my first favorites and still is.

Stress

Hansel, Tim. *When I Relax I Feel Guilty.* Elgin, IL: David C. Cook Publishing Co., 1979.

Hansel lives with pain all day, every day. In this book, he describes how to live in joy, above the level of mediocrity.

Hart, Archibald D. *Adrenaline and Stress: The Exciting New Breakthrough that Helps You Overcome Stress Damage.* Waco, TX: Word, Inc., 1988.

Dr. Hart identifies the activities and attitudes that people in our stressful world don't know how to cope with.

Suffering

Hansel, Tim. *You Gotta Keep Dancin'.* Elgin, IL: David C. Cook Publishing Co., 1983.

The personal story of Hansel's injury and pain—and the new perspective that helps him deal with it joyfully.

Roseveare, Helen. *Living Faith.* Minneapolis, MN: Bethany House, 1987.

The story of a single woman who endured incredible physical abuse as a medical missionary during the Mau-Mau revolutions in Africa, who was confronted by a question from God: "Helen, will you trust Me with this experience, even if I never tell you why?"

Sell, Charles. *Unfinished Business.* Portland, OR: Multnomah Press, 1989.

If I had one book to suggest on handling life's unfair assignments and old baggage from childhood, this would be it.

Smeades, Lewis. *Forgive and Forget: Healing the Hurts We Don't Deserve.* New York: Harper and Row Publishers, Inc., 1984.
Best overall book on practical forgiveness.

Wise, Robert. *When There Is No Miracle.* Ventura, CA: Regal Books, 1977.
Wise brings out the reality that everything in life is not magical. There is no magical answer to pain and suffering.

Yancey, Philip. *Where Is God When It Hurts?* Grand Rapids, MI: Zondervan, 1977.
Winner of a Gold Medallion Award, Yancey digs into the difficult problem of pain and suffering.

Working Parents

Grollman, Earl A. and Sweder, Gerri L. *The Working Parent Dilemma: How to Balance the Responsibilities of Children and Careers.* Boston, MA: Beacon Press, Inc., 1986.
Written by a rabbi and a child-development specialist, this book addresses the attitudes and problems of children whose parents work outside the home, with suggestions on how to shape those attitudes to help the children adjust.

Other Good Harvest House Reading

GROWING THROUGH DIVORCE
by *Jim Smoke*

Here is a practical guide for anyone facing divorce. This book can transform your life from an old ending to a new beginning and help to heal the deep hurts and doubts of anyone trapped in the despair of divorce. Includes a working guide to help you discover for yourself how to deal with the pain and develop new goals for tomorrow.

THE WORKING MOTHER'S GUIDE TO SANITY
by *Elsa Houtz*

Going beyond just identifying the problems, *The Working Mother's Guide to Sanity* provides answers, options, and solutions that work for the working mother. Filled with heartwarming examples and humorous anecdotes, Elsa Houtz shows the sometimes-funny, sometimes-trying, and always-challenging life of today's working mother.

GETTING THE BEST OUT OF YOUR KIDS
by *Kevin Leman*

Dr. Kevin Leman offers solutions to the toughest problems parents face. From knowing when to send little ones to nursery school to guiding turbulent teens through the pressures of drugs and sex, Leman provides penetrating insight and time-tested advice on raising kids from start to finish.

BEDTIME HUGS FOR LITTLE ONES
by *Debby Boone*

Written for children ages two to six, *Bedtime Hugs* is a unique collaboration by recording star and actress Debby Boone and her artist husband, Gabriel Ferrer. A collection of bedtime stories about many of the things children think about—growing up, dreams, the dark, shooting stars, being loved—it's written in a style that provides parents and children a rich opportunity to talk and share during the bedtime story hour. This storybook will be a favorite of parents and children alike.

GOD'S BEST FOR MY LIFE
by *Lloyd John Ogilvie*

Not since Oswald Chambers' *My Utmost for His Highest* has there been such an inspirational yet easy-to-read devotional. Dr. Ogilvie provides guidelines for maximizing your prayer and meditation time.

BEFORE YOU REMARRY
A Guide to Successful Remarriage
by *H. Norman Wright*

Before You Remarry is a creative study manual for couples planning to remarry. It overflows with important questions that encourage couples to think in-depth about love, marriage, the person they are planning to marry, and themselves. Exercises promote interaction and careful planning.

It covers such topics as • Readiness for remarriage • Love as a basis for marriage • Expectations • Goals in remarriage • Roles, responsibility and decision-making • In-laws • Finances • Conflict.

Dear Reader:

We would appreciate hearing from you regarding this Harvest House nonfiction book. It will enable us to continue to give you the best in Christian publishing.

1. What most influenced you to purchase *Sucessful Single Parenting*?
   - ☐ Author
   - ☐ Subject matter
   - ☐ Backcover copy
   - ☐ Recommendations
   - ☐ Cover/Title
   - ☐ _____

2. Where did you purchase this book?
   - ☐ Christian bookstore
   - ☐ General bookstore
   - ☐ Department store
   - ☐ Grocery store
   - ☐ Other

3. Your overall rating of this book:
   ☐ Excellent ☐ Very good ☐ Good ☐ Fair ☐ Poor

4. How likely would you be to purchase other books by this author?
   - ☐ Very likely
   - ☐ Somewhat likely
   - ☐ Not very likely
   - ☐ Not at all

5. What types of books most interest you?
   (check all that apply)
   - ☐ Women's Books
   - ☐ Marriage Books
   - ☐ Current Issues
   - ☐ Self Help/Psychology
   - ☐ Bible Studies
   - ☐ Fiction
   - ☐ Biographies
   - ☐ Children's Books
   - ☐ Youth Books
   - ☐ Other _____

6. Please check the box next to your age group.
   - ☐ Under 18
   - ☐ 18-24
   - ☐ 25-34
   - ☐ 35-44
   - ☐ 45-54
   - ☐ 55 and over

Mail to: Editorial Director
Harvest House Publishers
1075 Arrowsmith
Eugene, OR 97402

Name _____

Address _____

City _____ State _____ Zip _____

Thank you for helping us to help you in future publications!